FOREWORD BY GREG MOHR

MW00761433

GOOD FISH

BAD FISH

KEVIN CASEY

HOW TO HAVE ETERNAL LIFE,
LIVE A HEALTHIER LIFE
AND
AVOID THE WASTED LIFE

Touch the World
AUTHOR AWARD

ISBN-13: 978-1091004559

Good Fish Publishing

To the One who makes us Good Fish.

To the Bad Fish who want to change.

To the Good Fish who have learned how to fish.

Ken,
    I can't thank you enough for all of your help through the years. You have helped me to minister in a day where Visuals and design are the best bait in fishing for men. Thank you for helping me present everything with excellence—especially this new book.
    I love the light hearted packaging of this presentation of the greatest story ever told! Please agree with me for the lost, the new believer, and for churches everywhere discipling in small groups to be changed and helped by Good Fish Bad Fish! You are Amazing!

KG

This book, *Good Fish Bad Fish*, is a great resource for church members to reach out to their lost friends and loved ones. It exposes the lies many people hold on to that they are better than some so called "bad people" in their own minds and are therefore automatically saved and going to Heaven. It helps remove a performance mentality as a means of salvation and leaves the reader with no other option than to accept and believe on Jesus for their eternal life.

This is also a great discipleship guide that establishes a grace pathway for new believers to follow and grow into mature leaders in the Kingdom. It describes the significance of living a Spirit-filled life and being a part of a strong local church. The truth is, each of us has been made overcomers through Christ. *Good Fish Bad Fish* is an excellent manual on leading people to Jesus, learning to walk as overcomers, and becoming real disciples of Jesus!

Pastor Kevin Casey is a personal friend of mine I have known for over ten years. He is a great author and writer who has written a previous book on identity called, *Who's Your Daddy?* Kevin is a faithful pastor, husband and father of two awesome children. He has a passion for the truth and possesses a teaching style that is filled with humor and revelation. I know you will be blessed, challenged and empowered by the truths in this book.

Greg Mohr

Director of Charis Bible College
Woodland Park, Colorado

Thank you for picking up this copy of *Good Fish Bad Fish*. I hope you will be encouraged to know God through reading it. The purpose of this book is to help you come into a relationship with God through Jesus and begin to live for God's glory through the Holy Spirit's power.

As with my first book, *Who's Your Daddy?*, I would like to take a moment to point out a few grammatical liberties I took in writing *Good Fish Bad Fish*. I followed scripture's example by capitalizing "he" and "him" in reference to the Father, Jesus, and the Holy Spirit. I also did not capitalize the name of satan, even though it is a proper noun. I have included scripture references (unless used in a direct quote) in a series of endnotes listed at the end of the book for further study.

I am deeply thankful to the generous friends who believed in this message and helped bring it to print in this book. Thank you especially to Greg and Janice Mohr and Greg Mohr Ministries for their faithful friendship, consistent encouragement and for publishing *Good Fish Bad Fish*. Thank you to Melva Henderson, Pastor Mark Machen, Tonya Mohr, and Austin Smith for helping me to present the message truthfully and with clarity. Thank you to Jenna Drake-Garcia and her amazing team, especially Linsay Vladimirov, for their help making the message clear, interesting and bringing joy and encouragement through every page. Thanks to Marcus and Tricia Draper, also known as The Messengers, for providing the discipleship study guide at the back of the book. Finally, thank you to Kenneth and Lisa Logsdon not only for years of friendship and encouragement, but also for the cover design.

Table of Contents

Some things are too good to keep to yourself. That is the way I felt when I sat down to express the truth I have come to see as *Good Fish Bad Fish*. Having been raised in a home of faith, I have enjoyed life and have experienced great victories over some real trials and tribulations.

As an eight year old, I learned of God's heart and supernatural power when my mother was healed of breast cancer in 1974. The doctor was amazed as he looked at my mother's x-rays and then reexamined her to be sure he was reading the scans correctly. Perplexed, he called in a second doctor to attest to what he was witnessing. After deliberating, he confirmed that the tumor was gone. She praised God, telling her doctor, "God had performed a miracle." Cancer was a death sentence, threatening to leave our wide-eyed innocent family with a deep scar. Instead, it had lost its sting and the event became a monument in my life of God's goodness.

Nineteen years later on January 17, 1993, San Antonio, Texas was covered in a dense fog. My sister Karen was driving down Stone Oak Parkway and before she realized it, drove through the intersection of Highway 281. She passed over four lanes of traffic on 281 and collided into a rock and dirt embankment. A witness called 911 and emergency teams responded. She was rushed to the San Antonio Medical Center and slipped into a coma. Even after many surgeries to fix her multiple injuries, doctors still predicted she would likely only function with the mentality of a sixth grader.

My mom, however, heard in her heart while praying that Karen would be completely restored in ninety days. On April 12, exactly 85 days later, the staff applauded in astonishment as Karen walked the hall of the rehab facility without a cane or a walker. Only four days later, just shy of the 90-day promise, she would be released from treatment. Against the doctor's word that she would be mentally delayed, Karen later earned her second of two college degrees as a paralegal with a 4.0 grade average!

I have repeatedly heard it said that the Christian experience is one of ups and downs. Many say, "sometimes you may feel close to God, while other times you may feel distant and possibly forgotten." This is not my understanding from reading the Bible and walking with Him each and every day since I was a child. There are many in this world that still do not know the Bible teaches us the "Good News!" There is a way to live that is free, full, and meaningful regardless of life's circumstances.

The abundant Christian life is not just the dramatic, rah-rah moments of healing and prosperity, but the everyday decisions to follow God's voice and see His plan come to pass in every area of our lives. My family has overcome many storms of life including a few life-threatening accidents, financial challenges and other trials and tribulations that attempted to steal, kill or destroy us. Perhaps our greatest testimony of God's goodness is raising two children to be productive adults who are living life whole-heartedly following God and innocent of evil in a culture that often celebrates it. Whether difficult or victorious, these events only added to our testimony of the goodness of God.

While this way of life is available and free, it is not automatic. You and I must make a choice to live not just *for* God, but also *in* Him. In responding to His love and all He has done for us, you will experience what the Bible calls both abundant and eternal life. This is the message of *Good Fish Bad Fish*.

"Ready or not here I come!"

As a pastor I've had some great fun and memorable experiences with the people in my church. For instance, one early spring afternoon a man in my church asked me to go fishing at Eagle Mountain Lake with him. I was thankful for the opportunity, so we loaded up his boat with fishing tackle and headed to the lake. We cruised over the water with anticipation of a big catch and a relaxing time away from the day's concerns. The lake was pretty empty. With the sun waning in the afternoon sky, we quickly crossed through the dark green waters. Backing off of the throttle, we slowed our way into a quiet little bay. Immediately, we noticed some stirring in the water a little ways from the boat. The serene waters were coming to life as we hurried to cast our lines.

As soon as the lures hit the water, there was a familiar yank on each of our lines. With excitement, we quickly raced one another to bring in our catch. Both of us caught a healthy-sized fish in record time. We had never experienced a catch so large! We glanced at each other in amazement and excitedly cast our lines again, only to repeat the experience. We proceeded to quickly reel in fish after fish and after a short time, had reached our limit. It felt like we had caught almost all of the fish in the lake! I had never experienced anything like it, nor have I since. My friend joked with me saying, "I need to go fishing with the pastor more often!" That day left me with an unforgettable memory and a fantastic fish story.

You may have heard some fish stories like mine. Every fisherman has them. Even Jesus told a great "fish story." We find it in Matthew 13:47-51:

> *Again, the Kingdom of Heaven is like a fishing net that was thrown into the water and caught fish of every kind. When the net was full, they dragged it up onto the shore, sat down, and sorted the good fish into crates, but threw the bad ones away. That is the way it will be at the end of the world. The angels will come and separate the wicked people from the righteous, throwing the wicked into the fiery furnace, where there will be weeping and gnashing of teeth. Do you understand all these things?" "Yes," they said, "we do."*

Plain As Dirt

It's important to pause here and ask why Jesus used the imagery of fishing and fish to communicate as much he did. Unlike any other teacher, Jesus had a knack for putting big spiritual truths into earthly, real-life stories that were easy for his disciples to understand. He is speaking to people in a culture that grew up watching or being fishermen so he used these relatable narratives to reach their hearts with a higher, unseen but absolutely real, truth. Jesus also used these stories on repeat to emphasize their importance. In this Matthew passage, he says, "Again" because this is the *seventh* parable Jesus told in this portion of scripture about the Kingdom of God!

As the ultimate authority on this topic, Jesus told Nicodemus, a respected teacher of the law this: *"But if you don't believe me when I tell you about earthly things, how can you possibly believe if I tell you about heavenly things? No one has ever gone to heaven and returned. But the Son of Man has come down from heaven.*" (John 3:12-13). Jesus demonstrated an example of effective teaching by speaking from earthly, human experience that reveal an invisible but inescapable spiritual truth. This was not by accident. It had been prophesied that the Messiah would do this long before Jesus arrived.[1] Even for us today, this imagery can provide a powerful tool for understanding important spiritual truths.

The Harvest

The Matthew 13 story we just read about was not about a day on the lake, but to help us understand a day in the future that will happen. Jesus illustrated this future event using a fisherman's net. The fishing net is hauled in completely full of fish. Before this illustration, Jesus told a different story with a similar meaning. Instead of a net and fish, He used a field and the farmer's harvest to teach the principle that there would be a complete haul of the world. Jesus explains what this is by saying, "...The harvest is the end of the world, and the harvesters are the angels."[2]

No one escaped the harvest or the net. Fish of every kind were brought in: Red and yellow, black and white, rich and poor, the celebrities and the forgotten, those in republic governments and those in dictatorships, intellectuals and ignorant, moms and dads, and boys and girls—they were all swept away together for this moment of separation. When will this harvest take place? When the net is full. When the world is ripe.

---

1 "Jesus always used stories and illustrations like these when speaking to the crowds. In fact, he never spoke to them without using such parables. This fulfilled what God had spoken through the prophet: 'I will speak to you in parables.I will explain things hidden since the creation of the world.'" (Matt 13:34)

Psalm 78:2 for I will speak to you in a parable.I will teach you hidden lessons from our past—

2 Matthew 13:30; 13:40-43; 13:49-50; Revelation 19-22

Have you ever played hide-and-seek? When I was a child we would play games with all of the neighborhood kids. Hide-and-seek was one of the most popular games. It was a bit of an adventure for one person to close his or her eyes and count to one hundred while the rest of us frantically rushed to find the best place to hide. When the counter reached one hundred, he or she would call out, "Ready or not here I come!" Everything changed in that moment. We were no longer running around looking for the perfect hiding spot. The game had begun and he would then search until he found every one of us.

The Bible reveals to us there will come a time when the counting of days will end and Jesus will return for us. Ready or not, He is coming. If you are ready then you will enter into life. If you are not, you will be removed from His presence for all of eternity. He really wants us all to be ready.

Revelation, the last book of the Bible. foretells, "Then I saw a white cloud, and seated on the cloud was someone like the Son of Man. He had a gold crown on his head and a sharp sickle in his hand. Then another angel came from the Temple and shouted to the one sitting on the cloud, "Swing the sickle, for the time of harvest has come; the crop on earth is ripe." So the one sitting on the cloud swung his sickle over the earth, and the whole earth was harvested."[3]

There will come a time, a time set by the Father when the day of choosing will be over and the time of consequence will begin. Which type of fish are you? Where will you end up?

---

3 Revelation 14:14-16 *New Living Translation*

A Motley Crew Boils down to Two Types of Fish

Back in high school I remember students would identify with different social groups. As I matured I saw the categories change but the reality remained. We tend to separate into certain groups that have similar interests, experiences or passions in life. Although these groups are significantly diverse and some seem to be on opposite ends of the spectrum, the harvest of the world will reveal that there are really only two types of people on the planet. Jesus called them "good fish" or "bad fish." He tells us they were sorted by one difference for two drastically different destinations.

Jesus clearly explains *bad fish* will suffer eternally; "And the angels will throw them into the fiery furnace, where there will be weeping and gnashing of teeth." The *good fish* will enter into eternal life; "Then the righteous will shine like the sun in their Father's Kingdom."[4]

What makes a *good fish* good or a *bad fish* bad? It may surprise you to learn it is not about your good deeds out-measuring your bad ones. Instead, it boils down to how you answer this question: "What did you do with Jesus?" Did you reject His offer for life in relationship with Him or did you accept His offer and trust Him with your life?

A decision to trust Jesus must come from the core of who we are. It must come from the heart. Although we can hide our deepest thoughts and bluff our way through life before men, our devotion cannot be disguised before God.

---

4 Matthew 13:42-43

Chapter Takeaways:

1. We all are either a good fish or a bad fish.

2. Every person will face one of two drastically different eternal destinations.

3. Your eternal destination is determined by what you do with Jesus.

4. When you trust in Jesus and grow to know Him, He will affect your heart.

"The greatest disease in the West today is not
TB (Tuberculosis) or leprosy;
it is being unwanted, unloved and uncared for."
—Mother Teresa[1]

Once my wife Melanie and I went to a Christian conference at the Fort Worth Convention Center. There were thousands of people at the meeting and it was being televised. We were looking for a seat as the meeting was beginning. An usher told us to follow him and he led us through the aisle of pastors and ministers up towards the front. I thought, "Wow! This guy must think we are someone else" as we headed to the reserved seating area. He stopped and pointed to two seats on the very front row next to several ministry leaders that were affecting the whole world. I was not about to awkwardly correct his apparent mistake! We just smiled and thanked him. My parents had been attending that ministry's meetings for over twenty years but were sitting in the balcony; having never been to the front row before. We got the "very important persons" treatment and we did not mind one bit.

It was a bit surreal to be sitting with no one in front of us. When the speaker was preaching he got fired up and headed our direction. As he stood right in front of me we locked eyes and then he tapped my chest with his pointer

---

1   Teresa, Mother (1995). A Simple Path [E-book]. New York: Ballantine Books

finger. I actually flinched when he did. It is safe to say that being in that VIP position prompted us to pay very close attention to everything being said that night.

VIF

Did you know in the eyes of God you are a VIP? Or to stay within Jesus' illustration of the fishing net, you could say, "He considers you a *very important fish!*" God really does love you and He has a wonderful plan for your life. You may have heard that before but it is not an empty cliché from a sentimental Instagram post. God's Word guarantees this is true. Consider the words of the psalmist who wrote under the inspiration of the Holy Spirit when he said, *"How precious are your thoughts about me, O God. They cannot be numbered!"* (Psalm 139:17).

Our kids are now young adults. Through the years, we spent many hours going to the high school to watch them perform. Christopher plays the trumpet and so we always found the time in our schedules to go to his halftime performances at football games and seasonal concerts.

On each occasion that we arrived in the auditorium for a band performance, we would scan the arrangement of instruments to see where he was seated. We would then make our way through the hundreds of parents to find a good seat. You may be wondering, "What was a good seat?" A good seat was where we could see Chris the best. While there were hundreds of people in the room, we were there for our son. He is our VIP!

He graduated this past year and what once determined our schedule no longer does. We have not been to one high school football game or concert since. We were never there for the entertainment. We were there to celebrate our son, witness his accomplishments, and cheer him on in his expression of his interests. Jesus looks on you the same way.

Love Cannot Sit Still

God is love and He loves you, but many have never felt this love because their lives have been caught up in a convoluted mess of sin's consequences. Sin is the problem. Ever since the first man – Adam – it is everyone's problem. Adam chose to sin, but his children were born sinners. *"For everyone has sinned; we all fall short of God's glorious standard."* (Romans 3:23).

When we agree to sin, it hardens our hearts towards God and gives the devil an inroad into our lives. The devil's influence will always bring destruction to ruin your life and steal God's best from you. That is why the Bible says, *"For the wages of sin is death…"* (Romans 6:23a). The world without God is an environment saturated by sinful, hard, unloving hearts.

Someone may say, "If God really loved us then why is there so much suffering and difficulty? Love would not just sit passively by without acting to save a world of precious people made in His image." The most referenced scripture in the Bible, John 3:16, tells us God *did* do something and it cost Him dearly. *"For this is how God loved the world: He gave his one and only Son, so that everyone who believes in him will not perish but have eternal life."* (John 3:16). God did not just *say* He loves us. He demonstrated it through Jesus' actions. *"But God demonstrates his own love for us in this: While we were still sinners, Christ died for us."* (Romans 5:8 NIV). He not only died to demonstrate His love for us, He lived it. Everywhere Jesus went, He destroyed the devastation the devil brought against mankind. *"But the Son of God came to destroy the works of the devil."* (1 John 3:8b).

The devil hated God but could not attack the Almighty directly. He realized how important each individual man, woman and child is to God so he went after us with stealth-like vengeance. He legally tricked Adam out of God's glorious standard of a rich and satisfying life into a cursed one outside of a life-giving relationship with God. This destined mankind to share in satan's guilty verdict; incarcerating him into the same punishment of the inescapable eternal torment of hell. Jesus described this punishment as a, "fiery furnace, where there will be weeping and gnashing of teeth.[2]" Without hope of redemption, God's enemy tried to take God's children with him to punish The Most High God by hurting the ones He loved most.

Today, satan is defeated and the problem of sin has been fixed[3]. (That is a big statement that we will unpack and examine more in chapter four.) However, he is still hard at work tricking mankind and blinding them to God's plan of salvation[4]. If he can keep human beings from hearing and believing, he will legally take as many as he can to hell with him.

His tactic is to use the world's system that measures and compares us using a false appraisal; where we are evaluated on our net worth, natural abilities, appearance and popularity. Visionless of our own value in Father God's eyes, he leads us into destruction by elevating hollow, hurting people who do not make good choices into the limelight as examples of what we should be. But, when he is done with us, he quickly discards us like worthless garbage. Endless line of volunteers show up for this cruel abuse in search for their fifteen minutes of fame at the expense of an eternity in God's presence—enjoying His best.

---

2 Matthew 13:42
3 1 Corinthians 15:57; Colossians 2:14-15; Romans 3:24-26; 4:25; 5:17-19; 6:7-8
4 2 Corinthians 4:4
5 Marilyn Monroe's Quote http://www.goodreads.com/quotes/tag/celebrity

Consider the tragic words of Marilyn Monroe who is quoted as saying, "It's better for the whole world to know you, even as a sex star, than never to be known at all."[5] Officially, Marilyn died sadly of a drug overdose; broadly speculated to be a homicide[6]. Either version is heartbreaking for a child made in God's image but blinded by the lure of the world's praise.

> ...the world's applause is a poor substitute for our heavenly Father's adoration.

You may have felt ignored or over-looked in society. You may identify with the quote from Mother Theresa that "the biggest disease today is the feeling of being unwanted." You may have been passed over for a well-deserved promotion or recognition for all of your hard work. Or worse someone else may have gotten credit for your performance and received the acknowledgment or compensation for your hard work and investment of your time, resources and energy. Please remember, the world's applause is a poor substitute for our heavenly Father's adoration. You are His VIP.

Jesus lived only to honor His Father and would only receive honor from His Father. The world is full of VIPs that have no moral compass or eternal fruit in their lives. The devil's trick is to market and persuade us into living for inaccurate reasons, for the wrong glory and misplaced priorities ignorant of our value in Father God's eyes. The end result is a life full of distractions that amount to ashes in eternity instead of the rich reward God had intended.

---

6   Marilyn Monroe's Biography
    http://www.goodreads.com/author/show/82952.Marilyn_Monroe

Bad fish are hooked on chasing the lures of the devil; wasting their lives in pursuit of distractions instead of real living. Billy Graham said, "Many people teach that prosperity and a high standard of living are the highest goals attainable. The Bible teaches that materialism apart from God will destroy a nation as well as an individual.[7]" The apostle John reminds us,

The world is full of VIPs that have no moral compass or eternal fruit in their lives.

"Don't love the world's ways. Don't love the world's goods. Love of the world squeezes out love for the Father. Practically everything that goes on in the world—wanting your own way, wanting everything for yourself, wanting to appear important—has nothing to do with the Father. It just isolates you from him. The world and all its wanting, wanting, wanting is on the way out, but whoever does what God wants is set for eternity." (1 John 2:15-17 MSG).

The *good fish* has escaped the empty way of life and has begun to understand his value to the heart of the Most High God. Listen to John 3:16 again in The Message Translation as the meaning graciously reveals your value and importance to God:

---

7   Billy Graham - Read more at: https://billygraham.org/decision-magazine /december-2005/do-you-want-to-be-wealthy/

This is how much God loved the world: He gave his Son, his one and only Son. And this is why: so that no one need be destroyed; by believing in him, anyone can have a whole and lasting life. God didn't go to all the trouble of sending his Son merely to point an accusing finger, telling the world how bad it was. He came to help, to put the world right again. Anyone who trusts in him is acquitted; anyone who refuses to trust him has long since been under the death sentence without knowing it. And why? Because of that person's failure to believe in the one-of-a-kind Son of God when introduced to him. (John 3:16-18 MSG).

Jesus did all the work for you to be freed from the devil's lures and line. We step into life in Christ and away from darkness by simply believing that Jesus is God's Son and trusting Him as the Lord of our life. Jesus legally acted on our behalf to give us this choice to believe and follow Him through His way of life.

He paid a high price because you are His VIF (very important fish). Love from God paid for your ransom. He created you intentionally to *be* with abilities to *do* great things. His love now gives you the choice to respond to what He has done by freely swimming into that life of abundance and purpose.

Chapter Takeaways

1. Every person is a VIP in God's heart.
2. We need to be rescued from the life threatening consequences of a world saturated in sin.

3. The devil is fishing for men with a world of vivid, distracting lures to keep them blind to God's rescue plan.

4. All of us were at one time bad fish, but Jesus gave His life to show us our value to God and make it possible to be a good fish.

"O, my offense is rank, it smells to heaven;"
—Hamlet (Act 3, Scene 3, Page 2)

Bad Fish Stink to High Heaven

Shakespeare was describing a real stink. This was a stink that would not be easily overlooked or forgotten. It left a mark. I have heard this saying used as a country folk colloquialism. I do not know if country folk influenced Hamlet or if William Shakespeare influenced country folk but they both agree that if something really stinks it stinks to high heaven!

It is one thing to stink up the whole county, but it is another thing entirely to stink so bad you are recognized in heaven for it and suffer an eternity because of it.

God Knows My Heart

An evangelist who ministers in prisons told me he frequently asks inmates, "Who in here would say, 'I know I've done some bad things, but God knows my heart; I'm really not a bad person?'" He told me it is not unusual to see *every hand go up*. He then follows up with the statement like, "It is true that God sees your heart, that is the problem."

The Word says in Jeremiah 17:9-10, *"The human heart is the most deceitful of all things, and desperately wicked. Who really knows how bad it is?*

But I, the LORD, search all hearts and examine secret motives. I give all people their due rewards, according to what their actions deserve." Jesus also made this point when he spoke to those who tried to act religious but still had a hardened heart towards God. "Outwardly you look like righteous people, but inwardly your hearts are filled with hypocrisy and lawlessness." (Matthew 23:28). Bad fish may look good on the outside but their hearts still stink.

The evangelist goes on to tell the inmates, "You may hate me for telling you these things but I want you to know the truth, because then you can repent and be set free." He told me of one occasion when after he said this, a prisoner looked up with tears escaping from his eyes and called out, "You're not hurting us you are just loving us." It reminds me of the proverb that says: "In the end, people appreciate honest criticism far more than flattery." (Proverbs 28:23).

In the same manner, it's God's love that points out the true nature of our hearts. While behavior can be compared and measured against others, the truth is the heart is the source of your behavior[1] therefore God looks at and will judge us based on the condition of our hearts. A good fish has a good heart, and a bad fish has an evil one. Proverbs 24:12 says, "Don't excuse yourself by saying, "Look, we didn't know." For God understands all hearts, and he sees you. He who guards your soul knows you knew. He will repay all people as their actions deserve."

---

1 Proverbs 4:23; Matthew 6:21; 12:35; Luke 6:45; and Luke 12:34

Heart Attack

When Adam rejected God and chose to listen to the devil, an inward transformation took place. His heart became sick. It was broken and became hard and incapable of willingly following God. As mankind multiplied, time and time again his heart had proven it was disappearing into a bottomless sinkhole of rebellion. Genesis records, *"The Lord observed the extent of human wickedness on the earth, and he saw that everything they thought or imagined was consistently and totally evil. So the Lord was sorry he had ever made them and put them on the earth. It broke his heart."* (Genesis 6:5-6).

The Diagnosis Was Atrocious

The harder man's heart got, the worse his behavior became, as he was blind to his own rebellion. In mercy, God gave mankind the law, also referred to as the commandments. The law was given to expose our hearts to us[2]. It helped the spiritually blinded man to see the right kind of behavior a healthy heart would have.

A sinful, sick heart is unable to live consistently doing right things. When your heart is right with God and healthy, you will be compelled to live by love from the inside[3]. God's law revealed how a healthy heart would act since God's love would be in control instead of selfishness. In short, the indication that your heart is healthy is a life of actions that fulfill the law of God.

Proverbs 4:23 substantiated this, *"...your heart above all else, ...determines the course of your life."* So we see the law helped mankind who was now

---

2 See Romans 3:19 & 5:20; 1 Timothy 1:8-11
3 1 John 3:9 and 5:18

spiritually blind, to see they had a real spiritual heart condition that affected their whole lives. However, it just helped with the diagnosis; it did not help to cure the sick, sinful hearts[4].

> ...the indication that your heart is healthy is a life of actions that fulfill the law of God.

Jesus confirmed that the law was there to reveal what was wrong with us. But then He really turned up the light on our darkened condition when he said in Matthew 5:27-28, *"You have heard the commandment that says, 'You must not commit adultery.' But I say, anyone who even looks at a woman with lust has already committed adultery with her in his heart."* Where did the sin of adultery take place and where did it start? It all began in the heart. We understand Jesus was basically saying, *You may not have done the action but you are still guilty. Why? In your heart you did. Your heart, the deep center of who you are, is sinful. Mankind has a real problem. Your heart is sick and unwilling.*

The book of James further explains that sin is conceived in the heart and eventually it will end in death. *"These desires give birth to sinful actions. And when sin is allowed to grow, it gives birth to death."* (James 1:15). Jesus also revealed to us: *"For from the heart come evil thoughts, murder, adultery, all sexual immorality, theft, lying, and slander."* (Matthew 15:19). Even King David recognized he had a real problem that he could not fix when he said, *"For I was born a sinner, yes, from the moment my mother conceived me."* (Psalm 51:5).

---

4 Romans 3:20; Galatians 3:11

Every man, woman and child who is old enough to know right from wrong has been born into sin, has a bad heart, and is accountable for it. Billy Graham agreed that we all have a spiritual heart condition when he says, "The human heart is the same the world over.[5]"

To keep with Jesus' illustration of the *good fish* and the *bad fish* we now understand we are all born *bad fish*. That is why Romans 3:23 says, *"For everyone has sinned; we all fall short of God's glorious standard."* If you want to look at your heart to see if it is right with God then you have to look at it the way God does. How do we do that? We use His Word. Have you received a new heart or are you still living with the broken, sick one? This is a key understanding you must fix in your thoughts, "Look at my heart through God's Word to discover if I am right with God."

The Prescription

This is the condition mankind is in. But there is good news—*almost too good to be true*—good news! The reason Jesus came was to heal us from the inside out! He came to save us from our terminal illness—the *bad fish* condition. This was prophesied by Ezekiel when God said, *"And I will give you a new heart, and I will put a new spirit in you. I will take out your stony, stubborn heart and give you a tender, responsive heart."* (Ezekiel 36:26).

How would God accomplish this? Legally. If you place your trust in God it is comforting for us to hear that God knows our heart. We are encouraged: *"But when you pray, go away by yourself, shut the door behind you, and pray to your Father in private. Then your Father, who sees everything, will reward you."* (Matthew 6:6).

---

5   http://www.nytimes.com/1988/04/17/world/it-s-good-news-from-china-for-billy
    -graham.html

Jesus reassures us, one-day all *good fish* will be recognized and honored: Matthew 19:30 states, "But many who are the greatest now will be least important then, and those who seem least important now will be the greatest then.[6]" Have you thought about your heart condition? A *good fish* trusts God from his heart, and God sees the heart and knows the heart and that is what matters most.

Chapter Takeaways

1. Our thoughts, words, decisions and overall condition of our life grow out our heart.

2. All of Adam's children are born with a spiritual heart condition predisposed to sin. God gave us His law or commandments to help us diagnose our condition as sick, unable to obey God and headed for hell.

3. The law - telling us what is good or bad - was never intended to be the cure to our broken, hard heart.

4. Jesus came to heal our hearts. He changes us internally by giving us a new heart. This new heart has God's law written on it so we can choose to please God.

5. God's Word is the magnifying glass to analyze our hearts.

6. A good fish trusts God from his heart. God sees the heart and knows the heart, and that is what matters most.

---

6 See also Mark 10:31; Luke 13:30

I heard a funny story about a backwoods fisherman who was the only one in the town that could catch any fish. Every day he would come home with a successful catch. The game warden caught wind of this and was curiously suspicious. He followed the man the next day and watched him as he pulled out a stick of dynamite, lit it and tossed it into the water. After the explosion, fish began to float to the surface and he skimmed them into his net and boat. The game warden ran his boat up to the fisherman, and declared what he was doing was illegal and that he was placing him under arrest.

The old fisherman drew another stick from his pocket and lit it as the game warden was making his accusation. Then he tossed it towards the game warden who scrambled to catch it before it landed in his boat. The fisherman smiled and said, "Are you going to stand there and talk or are you going to fish?"

While this is a funny story, it reminds us there are laws and an authority in place that must be regarded. Our laws govern us in order to protect our way of life in this country. For example, one such law states that if you want to fish you must do it legally; and that means you need a license.

Every successful kingdom has laws. People want to come to the United States, for example, because of her laws and government not her mountains, prairies or amber waves of grain. There are majestic mountains and sparkling lakes elsewhere. Those who wrote the Constitution of the United

States sought to reflect the laws of the Kingdom of God; with biblical founding principles like liberty and justice for all.

Now the Kingdom of God is higher than any kingdom of man or even the laws of nature. God is a just God.[1] which means He does things according to the laws He has put in place. In order for the devil to get away with murder and for a "just God," who is also all-powerful, to be held back from doing anything, it had to be done through God's legal system. Satan, then, had to find a way to work within the laws of the Kingdom of God against mankind.

Origin of the Bad Fish Pathogen

The next few pages go in to some theological depth on the topic but stick with me as the information they contain is essential in understanding why things are the way they are and why God did what He did. Let's unpack this truth and examine it so we can receive and enjoy all of the abundant eternal life God desires for us.

In the beginning of our history God placed man in a beautiful garden and gave him the purpose of gardening. In Adam's garden, God and man had unhindered fellowship as God actually walked through the garden visiting with His children. They were *good fish* receiving only good things in life from their Good Father. Had mankind continued to cultivate the garden in tandem with God's blessings on their work, the whole world would have one day become a lush garden. There, unending fellowship with God would have been experienced along with generous provision for all of mankind.

---

1   Deuteronomy 32:4; Psalm 7:11; Isaiah 30:18; and 45:21

Instead, the serpent (devil), put this skill set to use by *legally* stealing, killing and destroying[2] all of the good God had designed for His children made in His image by getting them to agree with him instead of with God.[3] This was the *bad fish* pathogen that immediately spread to all of mankind since Adam and Eve were what we could call, "Patients Zero."

Jesus described the devil as, *"...a murderer from the beginning, and does not stand in the truth, because there is no truth in him. When he speaks a lie, he speaks from his own resources, for he is a liar and the father of it."* (John 8:44b). Moses chose the Hebrew word, "`aruwm`," to describe the serpent who deceived Adam and Eve. "`aruwm`" means, "subtle, shrewd, crafty, sly, sensible."[4]

It is very important to understand that when Adam and Eve sinned it was their choice to do so.[5] This meant there were consequences. They made a choice to *legally* act in agreement to go against God and agree with the devil. When they did this, they renounced all rights as children of the Most High and were *legally* swept away into the Kingdom of Darkness.[6] They died spiritually[7] and would eventually die physically. They were no longer righteous; meaning they were no longer right with God. Everything had changed.

Not only were Adam and Eve removed from immediate fellowship in the goodness of God but tragically, their children would also suffer greatly. The

---

2   John 10:10
3   Romans 5:12, 17-18
4   https://www.blueletterbible.org/lang/Lexicon/Lexicon.cfm?strongs=H6175&t=KJV
5   Genesis 3:1-19
6   Ephesians 2:1-3; John 8:44; Hebrews 2:14; 1 John 5:19; and Revelation 5:9
7   Genesis 2:17; Ephesians 2:1-3, 4-6; and Colossians 2:13

blessing God gave mankind to be fruitful and multiply had already been declared. Since God is bound by His Word, this meant men would increase as promised but they would be born into sin.[8] In essence, Adam and Eve *chose* to sin, but the rest of us were *born* sinners.

Although God still loved man and wanted to get things right between them again, it took some time before Jesus could come at just the right time to save mankind.[9] In the meantime, mankind had to be preserved. Since their hearts were hard, they could not understand their need to be saved. It was God's mercy that gave His people the Ten Commandments and all of God's law because it helped men to see their sick heart condition and look to God for help.

Another reason God gave us the law was to help us see the extent of our pitiful condition. We needed His standard because we were blind to our own failures. Romans 3:19 makes this clear: *"Obviously, the law applies to those to whom it was given, for its purpose is to keep people from having excuses, and to show that the entire world is guilty before God."*

Seeing sin or faults in others is easy—often too easy. However, when it comes to our own hearts, we are like the hardened prisoners, raising our hands while being punished for our crimes, saying, "I'm really not that bad, or at least I am better than a majority of others in here." The problem is we can't compare ourselves with others to be considered a *good fish*. Maybe we have not done the atrocities that other people have does but that doesn't indicate that we are legally and relationally right with God.

---

8   Psalm 51:5; Romans 3:19 & 23; 5:16
9   Romans 5:6 NLT

The Antidote

How would God make us right with Him again? It is essential to first understand that God's heart did not change towards Adam when he disobeyed God. However, Adam had legally broken his right position by following the devil and abandoning God. This presented not just a relational problem but also a legal challenge that had to be dealt with justly.

See, the devil had operated legally by deceiving mankind into rejecting God. Man's rejection of God was an illegal action that carried with it the death penalty. This rebellion is what the Bible calls "sin." Immediately, the life of man was turned over to the devil.[10] Satan was awarded Adam's dominion over the world,[11] and Adam was left with a toxic, sinful heart. Since he was the first man, this doomed all of his children, all of mankind to the same eternal punishment and separation from God.[12] Mankind had willfully chosen to follow satan, and as a result, died spiritually and was sentenced to share the devil's real, eternal punishment that awaits him at the end of time.[13]

Since the devil had attacked and stolen God's children and he had done it legally, he thought there was nothing God could do. However, God had a plan. Justice demanded sin had to be punished, but God knew that our hearts had to be healed, as well, so we could refrain from living as sinners again.[14] Sin had to be dealt with, once and for all![15]

---

10 John 8:44; Acts 10:38; Ephesians 2:2; Hebrews 2:14; 1 John 3:8 & 10 and Revelation 12:9
11 Genesis 1:26 and 2 Corinthians 4:4
12 Romans 5:18
13 Matthew 25:41 & 45
14 Romans 6:6; 1 John 3:6 & 9
15 2 Corinthians 5:12; Hebrews 9:26-28; 1 John 2:2

As stated before, everything God does is within the parameters of the laws He established. His ways are consistent and perfect. For example, the law of gravity is a perfect law that makes life possible on our planet. However, the higher physical laws of "thrust" and "lift" can be operated to help us fly around the globe. These laws take into account gravity and operate to overcome it. This is where it gets exciting. God used the law of love to overcome our rebellion and satisfy justice in order to restore fellowship with us. He would save mankind from a devil's hell, heal man's sick heart and demonstrate how great and real His love is for us.[16]

Gods' plan would be personally costly, but our great God of love considered the cost and lavishly paid it. His desire was to display His love in more than words, make things right legally between man and Himself, and heal man's heart so He could live right again. This would not only affect how mankind lived on Earth, but it also guaranteed a new eternal destination for those who would receive His gift of life. What God did to save us is amazing. He sent His Son, Jesus, to fix our mess. Instead of joining the devil in eternal punishment, we each have the option to be free from the sentence of death and live with God in eternal life![17]

So how did God's plan work, exactly? Throughout the Bible, we see that the blood of an animal or person is equivalent to their life. God gave Moses His law for the people of Israel. Through the law, sin was defined, and hearts were revealed as sinful. God also instituted a system of animal sacrifices where the blood was used to cover the sins of Israel. Leviticus 17:11 reveals this: "for the life of the body is in its blood. I have given you the blood on the altar to purify you, making you right with the Lord. It is the blood, given in exchange for a life, that makes purification possible."

---

16   Luke 4:18-19; John 3:16-17; Romans 5:8; 1 John 4:10
17   John 3:15-17; 36; 17:3; Romans 5:21; and 1 John 5:11

The law of God was broken by Adam and Eve's rebellion and justice demanded blood. Because of this, God became a man in Jesus and gave His blood in Adam's place. The Apostle Paul explained, *"Yes, Adam's one sin brings condemnation for everyone, but Christ's one act of righteousness brings a right relationship with God and new life for everyone. Because one person disobeyed God, many became sinners. But because one other person obeyed God, many will be made righteous."* (Romans 5:18-19).

Adam represented all of mankind. The first Adam lost everything. This is why God sent His Son to be the "Last Adam." Through His life, death and resurrection as a man He made it possible for mankind to be restored to a right place with God. The Scriptures tell us, *"The first man, Adam, became a living person." But the last Adam—that is, Christ—is a life-giving Spirit."* (1 Corinthians 15:45).

Love stepped in, legally, and paid the price of lifeblood to satisfy justice and to make it possible for all to be free from satan's capture and future punishment. You can now live from a new blood line, with a new heart, a hopeful future and a new heritage! Since Jesus was sinless His whole life He fulfilled the law completely in our place. The Bible calls Him the "Perfect, spotless Lamb of God."

Why a Lamb?

At one time men would deal with each other by giving each other their word. That became weak because men would lie and cheat each other. Next we would deal with each other, legally, with contracts. This is also weak. We found ways to get out of contracts or find a loophole in an effort to weasel out of our initial agreement with others.

God does not deal with men that way even though His Word can be trusted. He deals with men through covenants. Covenants are signed in blood and are permanent. In ancient times covenants were entered into through the sacrifice of an animal. In the Old Covenant, animals were sacrificed and their blood offered in order to cover the sins of those who had committed them. The priest would examine the lamb to ensure its perfection in order for it to be offered in the sinner's place. The priest did not examine the person, but rather looked at the lamb for flaws. If there were any defects, the sacrifice was rejected and the person's guilt would remain.

This was a real experience for the Old Covenant child of God, but it was also a picture that foreshadowed the truth: Jesus was our perfect sacrifice that was made once for all and was capable of removing our guilt before God. Father God used the blood of Jesus as the sacrifice to enter into a covenant with mankind to become right with Him again.[18]

But there is more to it. Jesus was punished in our place for our sins.[19] He was crucified to pay the price required to ransom men from the penalty for all of the world's sins. His perfection was given for our darkest, most tragic failures. Only the perfect, spotless Lamb would satisfy justice for man's rejection of God. Only His lifeblood was able to take away the sins of the world.

John the Baptist had this revelation. *"The next day John saw Jesus coming toward him and said, "Look! The Lamb of God who takes away the sin of the world!"* (John 1:29). The Apostle Peter explains further: *"For you know that God paid a ransom to save you from the empty life you inherited from*

---

18 Luke 22:20; Romans 3:25, 5:9; 1 Corinthians 11:25; Hebrews 10:22 and 12:24
19 Isaiah 53

your ancestors. *And it was not paid with mere gold or silver, which lose their value. It was the precious blood of Christ, the sinless, spotless Lamb of God."* (1 Peter 1:18-19).

There is a breathtaking, beautiful truth here. Under the New Covenant, the blood of animals does not cover sins; the blood of the Lamb of God washes them completely away. When we put our faith in Jesus, we agree that He is the sacrifice that makes us forgiven of all guilt. We are not examined, the Lamb is. He is perfect, and was offered in our place. Our best is not good enough but since Jesus never sinned, He is acceptable. This is why Jesus, alone, could pay the price for our forgiveness. No amount of good works or penance on our part could make us right with God.

> We are not examined, the Lamb is.

The Lamb of God became a man to die as a man so men could be set free from Adam's sentencing. The impossible had been done. Our sins were forgiven, but that is not all. The price had been paid with the life of Jesus for us to be adopted out of darkness and become children of God. We receive the benefit of His perfection. There was now opportunity for life to be restored.

> ...a part to play in this rescue plan that God could not do for us.

Jesus had done his part, but there was one thing left to do. Mankind had a part to play in this rescue plan that God could not do for us. We simply have to believe that what Jesus did was enough for our salvation. We have

Fishing Must Be Legal

to believe and trust Him with our lives. This act of trusting God is what the Bible calls faith. God's plan of graciously providing for us to be made right with Him is a free gift – but not automatic. We receive this gift by faith and grow to live a life of faith that affects every part of our lives.[20]

It is simple. We cannot become right with God by ourselves. This is why Evangelist Greg Laurie said, "Everybody needs Jesus. Have you realized that yet?"[21] Romans 3:22-28 says this beautifully:

> We are made right with God by placing our faith in Jesus Christ. And this is true for everyone who believes, no matter who we are. For everyone has sinned; we all fall short of God's glorious standard. Yet God, in his grace, freely makes us right in His sight. He did this through Christ Jesus when he freed us from the penalty for our sins. For God presented Jesus as the sacrifice for sin. People are made right with God when they believe that Jesus sacrificed his life, shedding his blood. This sacrifice shows that God was being fair when he held back and did not punish those who sinned in times past, for he was looking ahead and including them in what he would do in this present time. God did this to demonstrate his righteousness, for he himself is fair and just, and he makes sinners right in his sight when they believe in Jesus.
>
> Can we boast, then, that we have done anything to be accepted by God? No, because our acquittal is not based on

---

20   James 2:17-26
21   -@greglaurie
     11:02 PM - 28 Aug 2016 via Twitter

obeying the law. It is based on faith. So we are made right with God through faith and not by obeying the law.

One more time in Romans 3:30, Paul makes it clear that our part is faith that believes that Jesus did the work for our salvation. *"There is only one God, and he makes people right with himself only by faith…"*

The legal solution to mankind's *bad fish* condition and eternal punishment has been met through Jesus living a perfect life and offering himself in our place to pay the penalty. God could now legally give us right standing with Him, again, along with a new, clean heart that desires to stay that way. Our part is simply to respond to His generous grace, accepting His gift by believing in Him.

Have you believed in Jesus for His gift of life? When you do, you go through a transformation. Jesus called it being "born again." You were born into sin, but by putting your faith in Jesus, you are born again and receive a new spiritual heart, live by faith and overcome the world. We will look at the benefits of His salvation in our next chapter.

Chapter Takeaways

1. God is a just God and acts legally.
2. The devil legally tricked the first Adam into rebellion against God.
3. For Jesus to legally help mankind He had to live a sinless life and give His life, taking the punishment justice demanded for rebellion against God.
4. Jesus is called, "The Last Adam," since what He did could affect all of mankind.

5. Jesus did all the work for our salvation. This is called, "grace." Our response to God's gracious gift of life is to believe or have faith.

6. A bad fish can become a good fish by being born again.

"Fish are friends, not food."

—Bruce (The Great White Shark) in Finding Nemo[1]

In Disney's hilarious blockbuster movie *Finding Nemo*, Nemo's dad, Marlin, and his new forgetful friend, Dory, are searching the ocean for his son when they run into a Great White Shark named Bruce. Marlin and the audience expect them to be inhaled as tiny morsels past the rows of pearly smiling daggers that engulf the entire screen. Bruce, however, does the opposite. The suspense is broken when he explains to Marlin, with his deep, fear inspiring voice that he sees fish differently, now. Bruce is a reformed shark who has learned to view fish as friends and not as a snack (at least for the moment). Bruce's new identity made a drastic difference that saved Marlin's life. A believer has gone through a similar change. Our identity affects how we see and live in this world, but it also creates enemies.[2]

In the early days, after the birth of the church in ancient Rome, Christians were hunted down and persecuted mercilessly. They were thrown to the

lions and suffered as the Romans watched in their arenas of sport. It is believed that because of this, the early followers of Christ used a symbol[3] when meeting a stranger as

---

1   http://www.imdb.com/character/ch0003722/quotes - Disney's Finding Nemo 2003
2   Matthew 24:9; John 15:19; John 17:14; 1 John 3:13
3   Ichthus Image - https://en.wikipedia.org/wiki/Ichthys

a secret code for their protection to help identify one another as believers or to mark meeting places and tombs.

"According to one ancient story, when a Christian met a stranger in the road, the Christian sometimes drew one arc of the simple fish outline in the dirt. If the stranger drew the other arc, both believers knew they were in good company. Current bumper-sticker and business-card uses of the fish hearken back to this practice."[4] There are other hypotheses as to why the early Christians used a fish to identify one another. While the exact reason is unclear, it is historically true that the early believers used the fish as a symbol of their life's new identity, and they lived their lives following Jesus the Messiah.

The Root Changes the Fruit

When you give your life to Jesus there is a new way of life that is opened up to you. He is the "Author of Life"[5] and He will only lead you into real living. This is the type of living that begins today, but goes on forever. It is birthed and grows in a relationship. In order to bring this complete change, God changes our identity. No longer are we orphans outside of God's promises, but we are adopted and included in His family.[6] We are no longer called "sinners," but since we have been declared legally righteous before God, our identity is now in Jesus. This makes us a "saint."[7] We are no longer *bad fish* under the control of the devil; we are *good fish* compelled by love to live from our new identity in Jesus, the righteousness of Christ.[8]

---

4   http://www.christianitytoday.com/history/2008/august/what-is-origin-of
     -christian-fish-symbol.html

5   See Acts 3:15 NLT

6   Family of God – Romans 8:15; Galatians 4:6; Ephesians 1:5; 2:19; 1 Peter 2:17;
     1 John 3:9

7   Ephesians 2:19

8   2 Corinthians 5:21 KJV

Our new identity as a *good fish* renews our life's ambition to know God intimately,[9] and to receive all the benefits He paid for you to have as a child of God.[10] As we look into this, we need to keep in focus an often misunderstood but fundamental understanding for the follower of Christ. The Bible is separated by two covenants. As we briefly discussed in Chapter 4, there is the old covenant with blood sacrifices that was given to Israel through Moses, and the new covenant comes to all of us through the life sacrifice of Jesus on the cross. Under the old covenant, they were told what kind of fruit the child of God would have. The fruit was obedience to strict laws intending to keep them in spiritual, physical, relational, and societal bondage. Jesus said, *"Yes, just as you can identify a tree by its fruit, so you can identify people by their actions."* (Matthew 7:20).

> Our new identity as a *good fish* renews our life's ambition to know God intimately, and to receive all the benefits He paid for you to have as a child of God.

Under the new covenant the heart is changed so the fruit is possible. Before the cross, man's identity was in Adam. His life was rooted in Adam's sinful, heart condition. He was born that way. Therefore, he was unable to produce consistent fruit that pleased God. After the cross of Jesus, sin had been dealt with, and man could agree to be rooted in Jesus, whom

---

9   See John 17:3; Matt 22:29; Mark 12:24; 1 Corinthians 2:11-16; Colossians 1:10; Philippians 3:8

10   2 Peter 1:3 (NLT) "By his divine power, God has given us everything we need for living a godly life. We have received all of this by coming to know him, the one who called us to himself by means of his marvelous glory and excellence."

the Bible calls "the last Adam,"[11] and would naturally produce the fruit of righteousness. The new identity came with a new heart and promised new possibilities. Jesus called this being, "born again."

We can be born again into righteousness by trusting Jesus. The spiritual truth here is when you trust in Jesus for your life, God legally considers you to have died and risen with Christ.[12] In Father God's eyes, you join Jesus and you are raised as a new person.

This new heart has new programming. God's law was transferred from scrolls kept in the temple to the heart of man. Now you may live as the spiritual temple of the Holy Spirit.[13] Now you can own what the Bible says his children can have, do what it says they can do, and best of all, *be* who the Word says they can be!

> We can be born again into righteousness by trusting Jesus.

A child of God has God given rights. You are able to live actively in the promises of God and receive all that He is showering on us. God has promised we are healed, prosperous and full of the fruit of the Spirit including, love, joy and peace.[14] You may ask, "If this is true then why do we not see more of God's children enjoying His promises?" Just like a lamp must be plugged in to receive from the constant flow of electricity to shine, we have a part in receiving God's promises. God has graciously given

---

11   1 Corinthians 15:45-49
12   Romans 6:6 and Galatians 2:20
13   1 Corinthians 3:16 and 6:19; 1 Peter 2:5
14   1 Peter 2:24; John 10:10; 2 Corinthians 8:9 and Galatians 5:22-23

the promises of God. They have been paid in full and are live streaming 24/7 since the cross and resurrection of Jesus; however it takes faith to actively receive.

A good definition of faith is simply our positive response to what God has done. The Word tells us, the righteous live by faith.[15] The Bible calls the believer *righteous*, meaning Jesus made you right with His Father. The cross was a place of great exchange. He became our sin so we could become righteous by His sacrifice when we trust in Him. *"For He made Him who knew no sin to be sin for us, that we might become the righteousness of God in Him."* (2 Corinthians 5:21 NKJV).

He exchanged our position and our identity. Our new point of identity is hidden in Christ[16] instead of being in the past experience, in our job, or anything in this world that we use to define ourselves. We can now choose to live life as His Spirit lives in us to please God. The Apostle Paul said this, *"For God is working in you, giving you the desire and the power to do what pleases him."* (Philippians 2:13). Your job is to stay in the Word to renew your mind to who you are now.[17] This is why Reverend Billy Graham said, "Being a Christian is more than just an instantaneous conversion—it is a daily process whereby you grow to be more and more like Christ."[18]

> **Your job is to stay in the Word to renew your mind to who you are now.**

---

15 Hebrews 10:38a

16 Galatians 2:20; Colossians 3:3 and 2 Corinthians 5:17

17 Romans 12:2; Philemon 1:6

18 Billy Graham Quote - https://billygraham.org/devotion/a-daily-process/

Identifying Fish

Paul said, *"Examine yourselves to see if your faith is genuine. Test yourselves. Surely you know that Jesus Christ is among you; if not, you have failed the test of genuine faith."* (2 Corinthians 13:5). There are ways to identify fish in the natural. There are markers or unique outward features that help identify what type of fish you may be looking at. Examining their snout, spines, tail shape, body shape, and body patterns can help recognize and label the different species. Sometimes it may be fairly simple: If a fish has whiskers it is a type of *catfish*; if it has rows of very sharp teeth, swim the other direction.

There are ways to identify what Jesus called, "a good fish." Matthew 7:17-20 says, *"A good tree produces good fruit, and a bad tree produces bad fruit. A good tree can't produce bad fruit, and a bad tree can't produce good fruit. So every tree that does not produce good fruit is chopped down and thrown into the fire. Yes, just as you can identify a tree by its fruit, so you can identify people by their actions."*

What are the identifying markers of a *good fish*? How can we examine ourselves to see if we are in the faith? Here are some ways to help:

1. <u>You confess faith.</u> You cannot be "in genuine faith" without faith. God has given every man the measure of faith[19] because we have been made in His image. Genuine saving faith is confessed by the mouth and believed in the heart. What makes you a child of God is receiving by faith, what He has graciously given in Christ. A child of God believes and speaks.

---

19 Romans 12:3

The message of the cross is foolish to those who are headed for destruction! But we who are being saved know it is the very power of God." (1 Corinthians 1:18).

Since God in his wisdom saw to it that the world would never know him through human wisdom, he has used our foolish preaching to save those who believe. It is foolish to the Jews, who ask for signs from heaven. And it is foolish to the Greeks, who seek human wisdom. So when we preach that Christ was crucified, the Jews are offended and the Gentiles say it's all nonsense. But to those called by God to salvation, both Jews and Gentiles, Christ is the power of God and the wisdom of God. (1 Corinthians 1:21-24).

James tells us, faith without works is dead and that believing is not enough because even the demons believe and shudder (See James 2:19-20). The God kind of faith trusts in Jesus for life and living. Your confession is a basic action that makes the faith of your heart visible. Romans tells us, "If you openly declare that Jesus is Lord and believe in your heart that God raised him from the dead, you will be saved. For it is by believing in your heart that you are made right with God, and it is by openly declaring your faith that you are saved. As the Scriptures tell us, *"Anyone who trusts in him will never be disgraced."* (Romans 10:9-11).

2. <u>You have a love for the Word</u>. *'For the word of God is alive and powerful. It is sharper than the sharpest two-edged sword, cutting between soul and spirit, between joint and marrow. It exposes our innermost thoughts and desires."* (Hebrews 4:12).

The Bible says, a *good fish* has an inborn desire and delight or love for the Word of God.[20] This is a stark difference. The *good fish* has *affection* for God's instruction, but the *bad fish* has an *aversion* to it.[21] Although we have this affection, you must discipline yourself to learn the Word. As you prayerfully read this ancient book it will come to life and direct you in living from your new identity.[22] This is what the Bible refers to as "renewing your mind." [23]

Let's spend just a minute explaining a bit more about this concept of renewing your mind. Although we can be inspired by a scripture on its own, renewing our minds takes place when we spend thoughtful time reading, praying, and meditating on scripture. This is the way the Spirit brings the Bible to life to us. Truth is revealed and confirmed when we understand what was said, to whom it was said, and the culture the people lived in when it was written. Teachers of God's Word understand this as interpreting scripture in context. Another great rule for integrity in interpreting scripture is for a truth to be a real truth we should see it in at least two or three other places in the Bible. These simple practices keep us from making scripture say what we want it to. This is the way we read with humility and integrity letting the Bible transform us.

Jesus said, *"Not everyone who calls out to me, 'Lord! Lord!' will enter the Kingdom of Heaven. Only those who actually do the*

---

20 Psalm 1:1-2; 119:16; 1 John 2:5

21 Romans 8:5-10 NLT; 1 Corinthians 1:20-25

22 Romans 8:1; 2 Corinthians 5:17; Galatians 2:20, 6:15; Ephesians 1:3-4, 2:10 and Philippians 4:19

23 Romans 12:2

will of my Father in heaven will enter." Today, we are still faced with so many who say they love Jesus, but do not love His Word. (Matthew 7:21). The *good fish* lives in submission to the Word of God. This is where the rubber meets the road. If you say you love Jesus, you will live life yielded to His ways of doing things. This will change your politics, values, friends, passions and what you even enjoy for entertainment. He came to give you a rich and satisfying life, but He does not force that on you. He leads you through His Word, and you follow willingly.[24]

3. <u>You are led by the Spirit</u>. The Spirit of God lives in the *good fish* and will lead you into peace. The *bad fish* may hear from God because *"He does not want anyone to be destroyed, but wants everyone to repent."* But the *good fish* loves the inner witness and leading of God. (2 Peter 3:9b).[25] It takes time and discipline to unlearn listening to the devil, the flesh, and the world in order to hear the voice of the Lord. It is more a matter of turning down the volume of other voices of this world than convincing God to speak to you in order to follow Him better.

This is why every waking hour we are constantly bombarded with distractions that stream messages contrary to what God has said. The enemy uses the world to subtly captivate our attention stuffing our "ears to hear" with cares of the world. This chokes our ability to hear the Spirit's leading and the Word's influence to renew our minds. Only we can choose to change our focus.

---

24 John 10:1-14 especially verse 10
25 Romans 8:14-17

4. <u>You love at a supernatural level:</u> Jesus said in John 13:35, *"Your love for one another will prove to the world that you are my disciples."* He did not say, *They will know you are my followers if you are right all of the time*, or *if you have a revelation of grace and can point out everyone who does not* or *If you have faith bigger than everyone else in the room.* Rather, Paul said, *"Let love be your highest goal..."* (1 Corinthians 14:1a). Mother Teresa beautifully said, "It is not how much you do, but how much love we put into the doing and sharing with others that is important."[26]

    Love is supernatural. The Bible says it is God's identity.[27] As children of God, it is also ours. This world is living with a love for all the wrong things.[28] Only in Christ can you live constantly loving others as Christ loved us.[29] God's love in us causes us to forgive atrocities and be healed and whole as we live life to the fullest, the way God intends.

5. <u>Jesus is your Lord</u>. 1 Corinthians 12:3 *"So I want you to know that no one speaking by the Spirit of God will curse Jesus, and no one can say Jesus is Lord, except by the Holy Spirit."* Saying it means living it. A *good fish* recognizes Jesus as Savior, and worships Him as Lord. A *bad fish* is comfortable cursing His name, and is blind to his need for a savior.[30]

---

26 Teresa, Mother (1995). *A Simple Path* [E-book]. New York: Ballantine Books
27 1 John 4:8
28 2 Timothy 3:1-5
29 John 13:34; 1 John 4:7-8
30 John 8:43-45; 1 John 2:18, 22, 4:3 and 2 John 1:7

6. <u>You demonstrate the fruit of the Spirit and the character of Christ</u>. One's personality and passions begin to flow from the heart of God. The fruit of the Spirit will produce the character of Christ.[31] The longer you know Him and fellowship with Him, the more you will act like Him.

So examine yourself. Are you *a good fish* who understands you have a new identity in Christ or are you still a *bad fish* who may have cleaned up his lifestyle to look good to others but has never had a true heart change? God knows the heart. You cannot be good enough on your own.

Chapter Takeaways

1. *Good fish* have a new identity and their new life's focus is to learn who they are in Christ.

2. All of mankind was born into sin but believers are born again into righteousness.

3. There are ways to confirm and examine your new identity.

---

31   John 14:26, 16:13-15; Galatians 5:22-23

"God has privileged us in Christ Jesus to live above the ordinary human plane of life. Those who want to be ordinary and live on a lower plane can do so, but as for me, I will not."[1]

— Smith Wigglesworth

Once, while on a mission trip in Haiti, we prepared to head home after an awesome visit with Pastor Pierre and the people to whom he ministers. He has an amazing ministry to the rural people of Haiti where he feeds thousands beans, rice and the Gospel.[2] We were overwhelmed by the blessings, but also the starkness of things we had seen and experienced.

Since travel can be a bit complicated and unpredictable to a third world country, we planned on staying at a hotel close to the Port-au-Prince airport the night before we were to fly out. The hotel we were staying at was a surreal environment, seemingly a world away from the meager conditions we had witnessed that week in the villages.

The next day, we would be back home with the challenge of processing all that we had experienced—or so we thought. This was February 1999 and

---

1   https://www.goodreads.com/author/quotes/191049.Smith_Wigglesworth?page=1

2   www.lacroixhaitimission.org

American Airlines pilots had decided it was the best time for them to hold a "sick out," stopping travel.[3] As the days went by, our friends and family back home were frantically placing calls to our House Representatives, Senators and anyone who might have authority to get us back.

Meanwhile in Haiti, some of our team was beginning to experience some anxiety from several days without any answers or an apparent break in the strike from American Airlines. As a few of our courageous short-term missionaries were starting to emotionally meltdown, one of the men in our group came up with the brilliant plan of renting a boat for a short day excursion out into the Caribbean waters surrounding us.

Shortly after we began cruising through the waves under the tropical sun with the wind in our faces, the anxiety began to melt away. It was a generous gift that really helped the fragile morale of the team in a pressure cooker situation.

I swung my feet over the front of the bow and felt the water splashing them as our boat sailed. Suddenly, there were fish launching out of the water and flying for several seconds in front of our bow. I had never actually seen a flying fish, but there they were. I felt like I was witnessing a miracle.[4] They were not just jumping in front of the boat they were flying.

Flying fish live in tropical waters and have been recorded sailing up to 35 mph[5] through the sky up to four feet high and a remarkable 1,312 feet[6]

---

3 http://www.nytimes.com/1999/04/16/business/pilots-in-sickout-told-to-pay
   -airline-46-million.html

4 To view a flying fish in action:
   http://www.discovery.com/tv-shows/life/videos/flying-fish-fly/

5 https://www.nwf.org/wildlife/wildlife-library/amphibians-reptiles-and-fish/flying
   -fish.aspx

6 http://animals.nationalgeographic.com/animals/fish/flying-fish/

before returning to the water. The most accepted explanation for their exceptional trick of nature is that it is a defense mechanism to help them escape from prey. But the fish I witnessed just seemed to be living the all-day-fun, no-worries life of the tropics.

Soon after our miraculous boat ride that breathed new life into all of us, the pilots were ordered back to work and we headed back to the States. Though we were all thankful to finally go home, I would never forget about those flying fish.

God wants you to fly. He desires you to live the miraculous, adventurous life where the impossible is possible and lives are changed through you-like Jesus did. How will you live like Jesus did on this planet? The same way Jesus did: by the power of the Holy Spirit.

Acts 10:38 states, *"And you know that God anointed Jesus of Nazareth with the Holy Spirit and with power. Then Jesus went around doing good and healing all who were oppressed by the devil, for God was with him."* He not only wants you to do what Jesus did but even greater things.[7] He does not want you to just love your neighbor as yourself but He wants you to love them the way He loved you.[8] This takes supernatural power.

Jesus was fully man and fully God.[9] Yet, He operated with the power of God to destroy the works of the devil[10] and restore people to a healthy condition

---

7   Do what Jesus did and even greater things - John 14:12 & 17

8   Love like Jesus did - John 13:34; 15:12; 17:26

9   Jesus fully man and God - John 3:16; 20:31; Romans 1:4; Hebrews 2:14; Matthew 16:16-17

10   Jesus had the power of God to destroy the works of the devil - 1 John 3:8b NLT; Luke 13:16; Matthew 4:24; 8:16-18; 28-34; 12:28; Mark 1:32-34; Luke 4:41; 8:29-32; Acts 2:22 and 10:38

so they could live a rich and satisfying life.[11] Thankfully, He has already prepared for you to have the same power that Jesus did.[12]

Before the Cross

In the Old Testament, the Spirit of God would come upon men to do great works. Samson is celebrated today as a great body builder who could perform great feats because he was physically able to.[13] However, there is a reasonable argument that Samson did not actually have huge, hulk-type muscles. He was a regular guy who had been endowed from on high to exert great strength, in needful moments, to help Israel against her enemies.

Once he killed a lion with his bare hands. Another time he fought and killed 1,000 Philistines with the jawbone from the carcass of a donkey. Equally astounding was the time when he left a gated city in the middle of the night by simply lifting the doors of the city gates off of their hinges, and carrying them to the top of a nearby hill.

Since Samson could do things a normal human could not, it was obvious he had a supernatural secret. Samson had made a Nazirite vow before God. This vow was made in response to the direction of an angelic visitation to his parents before he was born. In order to be used of God, there were some stipulations as to how he could live. One part of this vow was that he was never to cut his hair.

---

11   Rich and satisfying life - John 10:10 (especially in the NLT)
12   Same Spirit on Jesus for the believer - Ephesians 1:19-20 NLT
13   Samson's story - Judges 13-16

In a romantic tragedy more famous than Romeo and Juliet, we meet Delilah, a beautiful temptress hired by Samson's enemies to seduce him into telling them the secret of his strength. While Samson slept, she sheered away his power. The enemy came to capture him, she sounded the alarm, and he woke to fight. Since he had broken his vow to God, the Spirit of God had left him; His power was no longer available. *"Then she cried out, 'Samson! The Philistines have come to capture you!' When he woke up, he thought, 'I will do as before and shake myself free.'* **But he didn't realize the Lord had left him.***"* (Judges 16:20. Emphasis mine).

His misplaced trust and her betrayal led to his torture and to the brutal merciless act of gouging out his eyes. Samson was powerless and humiliated, cruelly forced to do hard labor in prison. Then something started to happen again.

"But before long, his hair began to grow back." (Judges 16:22). Soon, the Spirit chose to come upon him for one last attack against his enemies. In his final act, he killed more than any other battle. Yet, he also perished.

Samson is only one example of how under the Old Covenant, the Spirit of God would come upon men in order to do great works with supernatural ability. Yet, the Holy Spirit did *not rest continually* in anyone because there was not a completely righteous vessel.

Jesus the First Righteous Vessel for Holy Spirit

When Jesus came, He fulfilled the law and lived a sinless life. He was the first and only one who lived perfectly and was right with God on His own merit. He earned His righteousness by being completely sinless. Finally, there was a righteous vessel for the Holy Spirit to come upon and work through.

This is why Jesus did not do any miracles until after His baptism when the Father audibly spoke His loving approval and the Holy Spirit descended upon Him like a dove. (Luke 3: 21-22). The first act the Holy Spirit did through Jesus was to lead Him into the desert for a time of fasting and prayer. Fasting is when you do not eat but turn your attention and desires all toward knowing God. I believe Jesus was learning how to live with the Holy Spirit working through Him to please His Father. At the beginning of the forty days, the Word says He was, "Full of the Holy Spirit"; after those days it says He, "returned to Galilee, filled with the Holy Spirit's power."[14]

It's important to take just a minute to understand the purpose of fasting in this process. I have experienced times in life, by my own choosing, of fasting and prayer. Ghandi went on a fast because the people were suffering. His fast brought the world's attention to the injustice and ended with change.[15] But Jesus' fast was not like that. When a believer fasts and prays, it is not to move God, but to *know God* and to turn down all of the world's distracting voices.

> Finally, there was a righteous vessel for the Holy Spirit to come upon and work through.

We see in this story of Jesus found in Luke, that Jesus was the first righteous vessel that the Holy Spirit could dwell in. He went into the desert, after receiving the Holy Spirit. He learned to allow the power of the Holy Spirit to work through Him to accomplish the things Father had for Him.

---

14 Jesus led by the Spirit finishes in the power - Luke 4:1 & 1
15 https://en.wikipedia.org/wiki/List_of_fasts_undertaken_by_Mahatma_Gandhi

Forty life-infusing days later, He returned to the Temple armed with the Power of the Holy Spirit to begin His ministry.

He began by claiming He was the fulfillment of the prophetic words of Isaiah:

The scroll of Isaiah the prophet was handed to him. He unrolled the scroll and found the place where this was written: "The Spirit of the Lord is upon me, for he has anointed me to bring Good News to the poor. He has sent me to proclaim that captives will be released, that the blind will see, that the oppressed will be set free, and that the time of the Lord's favor has come."

He rolled up the scroll, handed it back to the attendant, and sat down. All eyes in the synagogue looked at him intently. Then he began to speak to them. *"The Scripture you've just heard has been fulfilled this very day!"* (Luke 4:17-21).

His ministry continues to this day, restoring people's lives to health and obliterating all of the devil's work of stealing, killing and destruction.[16]

We Are Called to Live Like Jesus

Today, believers are called to do the same ministry Jesus did.[17] Many are trying to do it without the power Jesus used.[18] They have not even understood there is a way to live supernaturally.

---

16   John 10:10; 1 John 3:8b NLT; Luke 13:16; Matthew 4:24; 8:16-18; 28-34; 12:28; Mark 1:32-34; Luke 4:41; 8:29-32

17   John 14:12a; 17:18; 20:21; 1 John 4:17b

18   Same Power - John 14:17; Acts 10:38

Many are trying to do it without the power Jesus used.

The rulers who were under the devil and his demons influence thought they had defeated Jesus' plan.[19] They killed the only one who was righteous and put an end to His overwhelming power. There was nothing standing in their way now—or so they thought.

God's plan was to offer the perfect spotless lamb, Jesus, as a sacrifice that would satisfy justice and allow mercy to reign on mankind. The righteous one was sacrificed in our place so we could be made righteous not by our own works as Jesus was, but by faith in what Jesus did for us. His righteous place before the Father was earned; ours is a gift with privileges.[20]

Born of the Spirit

Jesus told a teacher of the law named Nicodemus that you must be born again. He was preaching a truth that was going to be fulfilled after the cross. Nic was perplexed by this statement as he considered the biological process of birth. Jesus then revealed that He was not talking about the flesh but a spiritual birth. *"Jesus replied, 'I assure you, no one can enter the Kingdom of God without being born of water and the Spirit. Humans can reproduce only human life, but the Holy Spirit gives birth to spiritual life. So don't be surprised when I say, 'You must be born again.'"* (John 3:5-7).

---

19 The devil was ignorant and influences the world - 1 Corinthians 2:8; Ephesians 2:2; 1 John 5:19

20 A gift with privileges - Acts 1:8; Romans 3:22-26; 5:1; 8:13; 10:10; 1 Corinthians 12-14; 2 Corinthians 5:21; Philippians 1:11; 3:9; 4:13; Galatians 5:16; and 2 Timothy 1:17

When a person hears and receives the Good News that Jesus gave His life so we could live righteously with Father God, there is a conception in his heart. When he submits his life willingly to God and recognizes with a faith-filled confession, the miracle of spiritual birth takes place. He becomes born again, this time of the Spirit.

On our church sign it reads, "A Spirit Filled Church." While this helps people to understand our church worship experience, it might disturb some believers. This is because all believers who know what the Word says understand that they are filled with the Holy Spirit at the new birth. As Romans 8:9 tells us you cannot be born again without the Spirit coming to live in you.

This is substantiated by the disciple's experience. After Jesus rose from the dead and appeared to His disciples who were in hiding, He breathed on them and said, "Receive the Holy Spirit."[21] This sealed them to the day of redemption as His.[22] The devil no longer had them. They were now righteous by faith in Jesus and Holy Spirit could now dwell in them continually.[23]

However, after this experience He also told them a peculiar thing. He told them to *wait* in Jerusalem and not to run out and tell everyone He was alive until the gift of the Holy Spirit had come upon them.[24] They would need power and boldness to confirm their message that the dead man named Jesus was now alive, and anyone who believes will be saved but anyone who refused would remain condemned.[25] Their message was true. The same power that Jesus operated in was about to be available to them in

---

21   Receive the Holy Spirit - John 14:17; 20:20
22   Sealed as His by the Spirit - Ephesians 4:30
23   Temple of the Holy Spirit - 1 Corinthians 6:19
24   Wait for the Baptism - Acts 1:4-5
25   If you believe you are saved – Mark 16:16

order to confirm the message was from God and to bring glory to Jesus.[26] This event took place in Acts chapter two, where the believers who were in Jesus were then baptized in fire as the Holy Spirit came. There was the supernatural sound of a mighty, rushing wind and appeared as tongues of fire to empower.

The devil was dealt a complete blow. Jesus had won. Now mankind had a choice to leave the devil's deception and destiny of eternal torment, and enter into life. The race was on to tell the whole world about salvation in Jesus, and the runners were armed with the same power that raised Jesus from the grave.

The enemy saw vulnerability in God's plan as he did with Adam in the garden, and deceived him out of following God. Since this new way of life still had to be taught in order for people to learn about it,[27] the Achilles heel was to keep the messengers from spreading the message, or at the very least, to confuse the message.

> **The race was on to tell the whole world about salvation in Jesus, and the runners were armed with the same power that raised Jesus from the grave.**

Today, there is ignorance of this imperative part of the Good News for mankind. Paul faced it as he ran to preach the grace of God through Jesus' sacrifice and faith in Him for receiving and living for Him. Once while visiting

---

26 Signs confirmed the message – Mark 16:20; Acts 14:3; Hebrews 2:4
27 How will they know - Romans 10:14-15

a city, he heard some runners telling the Good News but not the complete message. In ignorance, they only knew of repentance of sin. The Message version beautifully describes this event:

> Now, it happened that while Apollos was away in Corinth, Paul made his way down through the mountains, came to Ephesus, and happened on some disciples there. The first thing he said was, "Did you receive the Holy Spirit when you believed? Did you take God into your mind only, or did you also embrace him with your heart? Did he get inside you?" "We've never even heard of that—a Holy Spirit? God within us?" "How were you baptized, then?" asked Paul.
>
> "In John's baptism." "That explains it," said Paul. "John preached a baptism of radical life-change so that people would be ready to receive the One coming after him, who turned out to be Jesus. If you've been baptized in John's baptism, you're ready now for the real thing, for Jesus."
>
> And they were. As soon as they heard of it, they were baptized in the name of the Master Jesus. Paul put his hands on their heads and the Holy Spirit entered them. From that moment on, they were praising God in tongues and talking about God's actions ("spoke in tongues and prophesied" are used in New Living Translation). Altogether there were about twelve people there that day. (Acts 19:1-7).

Throughout the book of Acts, we see the fulfillment of Jesus promise for power to confirm the message. Yet so many believers today are still in ignorance about the baptism of the Holy Spirit. Even worse, many have been taught a doctrine from trusted pulpits that this has passed away.

They've been taught that the power of God is possible but unpredictable, and that it may or may not show up. This teaching has kept them looking godly, but lacking power to help people believe the Word.

In the early church history recorded in Acts, we find that being baptized in the Holy Spirit was part of the salvation experience.[28] So was water baptism. Today, many churches hold special services to water baptize new believers. This is only for logistic reasons. It takes three to four hours to fill our church baptistry with fresh water. This makes it impractical to do every time there is a response to the Gospel.

Many believers today are still in ignorance about the baptism of the Holy Spirit.

However, in the scriptures people were immediately baptized in water after making a public confession of faith. We all agree that this is important because it is an action you willingly and publicly participate in, it identifies you as a believer in Christ, and is your first opportunity to witness to the world that Jesus is your Lord.[29] It is difficult to overstate the beauty and power of a public profession of faith that is made when a person is water baptized. The kingdom of darkness that influences this world understands this and persecutes believers for coming out publicly. Water baptisms are punished by imprisonment and death throughout the world. The casual observer may wonder at the cruel irrational response to this seemingly simple action. However, it demonstrates the Kingdom of God taking over

---

28   Acts 10:38-48 NLT
29   Romans 6:4; Romans 6:3-11 MSG; Galatians 3:26-27; Colossians 2:12

where the kingdom of darkness once ruled. Water baptism proclaims your new identity. Heaven celebrates, but darkness trembles and hates to see new believers take a bold stand for God.

We call baptisms separate experiences. While in scripture we see they worked in tandem with the Gospel being preached, sinners repenting and believing on Jesus for eternal life. The Holy Spirit baptizing new believers in power and heading to the river to publicly identify with Christ are integral parts of the process. Although the church has taught these are all separate experiences, God's heart is clear. He wants every new believer to publicly proclaim that Jesus is their Lord and fill them with the power they need to witness and live for Christ soon after responding to the Gospel!

It is no mistake that Jesus said, "you must be born again, by the Spirit."[30] The natural flesh was a picture of a supernatural work of the Spirit. When a baby is born, water breaks and the first thing the infant does is breathe in his or her first great breath. When a person is born again, part of the process is to receive the Spirit,[31] and learn to let Him lead. He brings gifts and will produce the fruit of the Spirit,[32] which is the nature and character of Christ. Likewise, water baptism is what we do in response to what He has done as a part of the beauty of coming to life.

Once the church began to pull apart the process of the new birth and empowerment for living, denominations began to discount or elevate baptisms beyond what was intended. In short, God looks at the heart, and His

---

30 John 3:5-7

31 The Greek word in scripture "Pneuma" is interpreted "Spirit" meaning "breath of nostrils or mouth" but also "the third person of the triune God, the Holy Spirit, coequal, coeternal with the Father and the Son" https://www.blueletterbible.org/lang/Lexicon/Lexicon.cfm?strongs=G4151&t=KJV

32 Romans 12, 1 Corinthians 12-14 and Galatians 5:22-23

work at the cross is complete. Our response is to believe. Water baptism is faith in action. Holy Spirit baptism is the supernatural confirmation and empowerment to help you follow Christ. Without it, you are swimming upstream on the power of your own determination. With it, you are launching into the air like those flying fish in Haiti, to do what Christ did and even greater things.

Someone may ask, "Will I be considered a *good fish* if I was never water baptized before I passed from this life?" The Word teaches clearly that we put our faith in Jesus' work plus nothing else. We are right with Father God because of what Jesus did and our response of faith in Him allows us to immediately receive what He has freely given. Romans 10:10 tells us, "For it is by believing in your heart that you are made right with God, and it is by openly declaring your faith that you are saved." He did all of the heavy lifting for our salvation. However, this new life of faith means you are living a new life of obedience. As a child of God you will *want* to identify with Christ. You will *desire* to be water baptized.

What about the Holy Spirit's baptism? When a child of God comes to life in the Kingdom he needs to be empowered to live a victorious life that witnesses about God.[33] The baptism of the Holy Spirit is how God chose to do this. When you are Spirit led a whole new way of power and protection is available. Without it you will still go on to eternal life, but living and ministering in your own strength or determination is exhausting and all of your self-effort may end up sending you to heaven sooner than you needed to go.

---

33   Acts 1:8

Fish Are Not Supposed to Fly

Fish are made to swim but the flying fish does both. There is something inside the flying fish that sets him apart from other fish. As he swims towards the surface of the water with great speed, something inside of him causes him to aim higher and he launches out of the big blue into greater things! No one knows what triggers him to propel to greater heights than other fish.

There is a trigger in your heart after you have been baptized in the Holy Spirit. We see in the book of Acts that it accompanied the baptism of the Holy Spirit.[34] When the believer speaks or prays in tongues he builds himself up in faith and keeps himself in the love of God.[35] It is the trigger that propels the believer into the influence of the Holy Spirit's power into their lives or circumstances.

When you pray in tongues your mind is not built up or encouraged; you do not know what you are saying.[36] Rather, you are bypassing the weakness of your mind that may be hindered by ignorance, unbelief, the world, the flesh, or the devil. Instead, the Word tells us you are praying the perfect will of God. It is a beautiful gift that offends the flesh because it cannot understand. This is why the world and believers who are dominated by the flesh in their understanding make cynical, unbelieving jokes or refuse to believe it is real.[37]

---

34 Many occasions where believers were baptized in the Holy Spirit the supernatural evidence was the gift of tongues – Acts 2:1-4; 8:19 Peter laid hands on the new believers and the power was given, Simon saw something supernatural happened. Acts 10:44-46; 19:6

35 1 Corinthians 14:4; Jude 20-21

36 1 Corinthians 14:4; Romans 8:26-27; Ephesians 6:18

37 Romans 8:5-7

In short, Flying Fish cannot be understood by regular fish, but they will do greater things than can be done by their own strength. As believers, God has graciously paid for us to receive His supernatural power to live like Jesus did.[38] We cannot receive if we do not believe. This is why the devil must fight so hard to discourage, confuse or convince God's Saints to refuse His promise of empowerment. It is much more profitable in the Kingdom of God to live with His strength and ability instead of mustering up your own will and determination to follow Him.

Today many in the church are buying into the lie that our great hope, once we receive Christ as our Savior, is to endure here and shy away from being identified as different in order to avoid persecution. Many churches and ignorant church folks out in the world are not preaching the true Gospel or refuse to give opportunity for the Holy Spirit to work. As a result, there are few healings or miracles and other evidences of the power of God. Too many believers are hiding in their bunkers watching the world slide into a decrescendo of darkness asking, "Where it would all end?"

> Today many in the church are buying into the lie that our great hope, once we receive Christ as our Savior, is to endure here

The church in her early days depended on the influence of the Holy Spirit for living and ministering. In those days, the church was bold and effective. It is not coincidence that the book in which the Bible records the birth

---

38   John 17:18; 20:21; 1 John 4:17b

of the church is titled, "Acts." The Word was preached, Jesus' love was expressed and people encountered the power of God's Holy Spirit. It was normal Christianity. They did not wring their hands and hide, wondering where it would all end. It was the enemies of the growing church that were fearful of the power of God and "...*were perplexed, wondering where it would all end"* (Acts 5:24b)

Today, the church has been guilty of discounting the power and role of the Holy Spirit and in so doing keeps the Holy Spirit dormant in our lives and ministry. Whether because of ignorance or trying to be more palatable to the world, we've ended up exactly opposite of where we started. Once it was enemies of the church being threatened and fearful of the power of God and wondering, "when is this going to end." Sadly, these days it's many Christians living in defeat and fear of what may happen. They passively mark time barely holding on until Jesus' return, hoping to take care of their needs but go unnoticed while here in the world.

In the Old Covenant or Old Testament, God's children did not have the promise of the Holy Spirit's constant abiding presence and power. As the righteousness of Christ after the finished work of the cross, the presence is always in us and the baptism of the Holy Spirit is available. As such, it is time for the message to be complete and clear. We believers must minister and live depending on the Holy Spirit. We must educate our hearts and minds to depend on Him for effectiveness! We must preach the message He endorses with His power! We must realize His role is to glorify Jesus in each of us, not to make us celebrities in the world!

Without depending on His influence and power, you can live for Jesus and swim through the currents of the world. However, once you yield and embrace all He has for you, you can launch into doing greater things and fly with power to confirm the Good News, heal the broken hearted, proclaim sight to the blind, set captives free, and live in joy during the year of the Lord's favor, accomplishing Father God's will, and by bringing glory to Jesus by the power of the Holy Spirit! These are the things Jesus did and what He has commissioned the church to continue doing. (See Luke 4:18-19; Isa 61:1-2a; Mark 16:15-20; John 14:12; Matt 28:18-20; Acts 1:8)

Kathryn Kuhlman was a minister in the 1970s that was renowned for powerful miracles in her meetings. My parents went to one of her meetings and experienced first-hand the sick being made whole throughout the service and all around them. My dad told me of one woman in particular who stood up beside them worshipping God with cloudy tears running down her cheeks. She was experiencing the power of God melting the cataracts right out of her eyes. She wept as her cataracts disappeared and her sight became clear again.

Kathryn Kuhlman gave honor to the Holy Spirit for these prolific miracles in her meetings. She revealed the reason for such amazing miracles when she said, "I surrendered unto Him all there was of me, everything! Then I realized what it meant for the first time to have real power."[39]

Chapter Takeaways

1. God has called the believer to do the things Jesus did and even greater things.

2. Holy Spirit's power was available to some for specific instances in the Old Covenant but would not constantly remain on them because no one was righteous.

3. Jesus was righteous on His own merit and the Holy Spirit was able to rest on Him empowering Him to do the things He did.

---

39 http://godsgenerals.com/

Jesus made the believer righteous, legally, therefore we are sealed with the Holy Spirit's presence in our hearts.

4. Holy Spirit's power is available to us to do the things Jesus did and even greater things. Some do not operate in power because they are ignorant of His priority in ministry and have become self-dependent instead of Holy Spirit dependent. Another reason is that they are not preaching a message He endorses—His job is to bring glory to Jesus.

Chapter 7 — Deceived Fish

"My heart aches for America and its deceived people."

— Billy Graham[1]

Frequently, I will ask a hypothetical question to people who have given me a voice in their lives. "If you were to die today and face Jesus at heaven's pearly gates what would you say to Him if He asked you, "Why should I let you in?" Many times, they will answer me after a quick mental evaluation, "Well, I've done more good things than bad," "I have been a good husband or father," or, "I did my best and did better than a lot of people I know."

Those answers reveal a dangerous deception that the people of Israel also shared and Paul grieved over. Your answer should not be about *what you have done* but that you are *trusting in what Jesus has done*.

This deception is prevalent in our society, leaving us to be concerned that our loved ones are trusting in themselves, and they are *bad fish* who think they are *good fish*. Their destiny is hell. I have heard minister and author Andrew Wommack say it perfectly, "You may be better than the next guy, but who wants to be the best sinner in hell?"

Throughout the history of the church, there have been deceived teachers who come in to lead the *good fish* into deception, division and darkness.

---

1   https://billygraham.org/story/billy-graham-my-heart-aches-for-america/

This happened in the apostle Paul's day, and it is still going on today.[2] Jesus told a parable about wheat and weeds.[3] In this story, the field was growing well, but at night the enemy came in and sowed seeds of weeds. The weeds grew and looked just like wheat externally, but they were inedible. At the harvest they are separated—one is destroyed while the other enters into life —a foreboding reinforcement of the *good fish* and *bad fish* scenario.

Jesus identified deceived fish for us: "What sorrow awaits you teachers of religious law and you Pharisees. Hypocrites! For you are like whitewashed tombs—beautiful on the outside but filled on the inside with dead people's bones and all sorts of impurity. (Matthew 23:27). Jesus also called them "blind guides" in Matthew 15:13-14: "Jesus replied, 'Every plant not planted by my heavenly Father will be uprooted, so ignore them. They are blind guides leading the blind, and if one blind person guides another, they will both fall into a ditch.'"

One type of deceived fish is someone who thinks they are a *good fish*, but they have not responded to God's gift of salvation offered through Christ. They look good on the outside, but they have sought to establish their own righteousness instead of receiving Jesus'.

Paul grieved for the deceived of Israel when he said, *"For they don't understand God's way of making people right with himself. Refusing to accept God's way, they cling to their own way of getting right with God by trying to keep the law. For Christ has already accomplished the purpose for which the law was given. As a result, all who believe in him are made right with God."* (Romans 10:3-4).

---

2   Philippians 1:15-18; 1 Timothy 6:3-5; Titus 3:10-11; Jude 1:4 and 18-19
3   Matthew 13:24-30

He goes on and preaches the simple message: to turn from your ways of trying to be right and receive Jesus' gift of righteousness. You cannot do both. Salvation is not a reward for living better than the next guy. Just as a tree produces fruit because it is a fruit tree, believers will act right because they believe in Jesus to be right. Legally, you cannot act right to be right with God; you have to believe in Jesus and what He did for you to be right, which causes you to act right.

> If you openly declare that Jesus is Lord and believe in your heart that God raised him from the dead, you will be saved. For it is by believing in your heart that you are made right with God, and it is by openly declaring your faith that you are saved. As the Scriptures tell us, "Anyone who trusts in him will never be disgraced." Jew and Gentile are the same in this respect. They have the same Lord, who gives generously to all who call on him. For "Everyone who calls on the name of the Lord will be saved." (Romans 10:9-13)

Sometimes It's Hard to Tell

There is a difference between a *bad fish* and a *good fish* that has fallen into sin. Consider these passages where the Apostle Paul warned the believer in regards to being free from sin and then flirting with it all over again: *"Well then, should we keep on sinning so that God can show us more and more of his wonderful grace? Of course not! Since we have died to sin, how can we continue to live in it?"* (Romans 6:1-2). Later on in verses six and seven the author states, *"We know that our old sinful selves were crucified with Christ so that sin might lose its power in our lives. We are no longer slaves to sin. For when we died with Christ we were set free from the power of sin."* (Romans 6:6-7).

There is a difference between a *bad fish* and a *good fish* that has fallen into sin.

Romans 6:15-18 continues: *"Well then, since God's grace has set us free from the law, does that mean we can go on sinning? Of course not! Don't you realize that you become the slave of whatever you choose to obey? You can be a slave to sin, which leads to death, or you can choose to obey God, which leads to righteous living. Thank God! Once you were slaves of sin, but now you wholeheartedly obey this teaching we have given you. Now you are free from your slavery to sin, and you have become slaves to righteous living."*

Eugene Peterson is a minister who translated the Bible into modern common English. The result is called The Message, which communicates the Good News beautifully. Listen to his translation of the Apostle Paul's words with your heart as it clearly describes how a *good fish* or believer should live in these late times of history preparing for the imminent harvest Jesus warned us about:

> *But make sure that you don't get so absorbed and exhausted in taking care of all your day-by-day obligations that you lose track of the time and doze off, oblivious to God. The night is about over, dawn is about to break. Be up and awake to what God is doing! God is putting the finishing touches on the salvation work he began when we first believed. We can't afford to waste a minute, must not squander these precious daylight hours in frivolity and indulgence, in sleeping around and dissipation, in bickering and grabbing everything in sight. Get out of bed and get dressed! Don't loiter and linger, waiting until the very last minute. Dress yourselves in Christ, and be up and about!* (Romans 13:11-14 MSG).

The problem of sin has been dealt with legally through the blood of Jesus. Hebrews 9:28 says, "so also Christ was offered once for all time as a sacrifice to take away the sins of many people. He will come again, not to deal with our sins, but to bring salvation to all who are eagerly waiting for him."

If the believer chooses to sin, however, he should repent. Repentance means reverse or change your thinking in an area. Repentance begins with a decision, but it is also a process of walking it out as you renew your mind to God's Word. Some raise their hands in a moment to repent publicly, but then go right back to living in sin. Why? Because it is a master that does not want to let go.

Be encouraged to know that the power that raised Christ from the dead is in you, helping you renounce the sin that so easily entangles you, and then sending you into freedom.[4] It is a dead foe that has been defeated. The only real power it holds is deception. This is very important to understand so that we don't focus only on ourselves and our sin.

With that said, it is also important to spend just a bit of time really understanding the effects of sin. Peter said, worldly desires will, "War against your soul."[5] Sin affects us in three primary ways: It hardens your heart toward God, affects your witness of Jesus to others, and gives the devil an entrance to steal, kill and destroy your life. When we repent, it brings life. We receive God's forgiveness, and we walk free from condemnation in order to live free from deception that paralyzes us. This is a watchful balance of realizing God's life is a free gift. You must receive it, and not

---

4   John 14:17; Romans 8:9-10, 11 and 15; 1 Corinthians 3:16; Galatians 5:16-18; Ephesians 4:22-24; 1 John 2:27; 1 john 4:4 and Hebrews 12:1-4

5   1 Peter 2:11 (NLT)
      11 Dear friends, I warn you as "temporary residents and foreigners" to keep away from worldly desires that wage war against your very souls.

frustrate His grace towards your life by trying to earn your freedom by looking to yourself.[6]

It is also true that you cannot receive this grace without a faith that acts. In order for you to be free, you must submit to God's Word. This will require discipline to *prayerfully read*, *believe* and *resist* the fear that may press your heart by using the diminishing voice of past experiences to move you back to the slavery of sin.

Today, there is a strange, toxic, and deceptive belief once again creeping into the church, that God's grace somehow makes it *possible to sin* instead of *impossible* for the believer. This deception lures the believer into thinking the pleasures of sin are possible, while enjoying the pleasures of God. This leaves us double minded and unstable.[7] This is nothing new. The Book of Jude describes clearly: *"I say this because some ungodly people have wormed their way into your churches, saying that God's marvelous grace allows us to live immoral lives. The condemnation of such people was recorded long ago, for they have denied our only Master and Lord, Jesus Christ."* (Jude 4)

Billy Graham reveals the heart of this problem in the

> Today, there is a strange, toxic, and deceptive belief once again creeping into the church, that God's grace somehow makes it *possible to sin* instead of *impossible* for the believer.

---

6   Galatians 2:21 KJV; Romans 10:3 KJV
7   James 1:8

church when he said, "Those outside the church expect followers of Christ to live differently, yet today many in church are chasing after the world — not to win them, but to be like them."[8] Jesus said you could not serve two masters: *"No one can serve two masters. For you will hate one and love the other; you will be devoted to one and despise the other..."* (Matthew 6:24a). In fact, grace makes it possible to be done with sin. 1 John 3:9-10 states, *"Those who have been born into God's family do not make a practice of sinning, because God's life is in them. So they can't keep on sinning, because they are children of God. So now we can tell who are children of God and who are children of the devil. Anyone who does not live righteously and does not love other believers does not belong to God."* Again, I heard Andrew Wommack once say, "It does not mean that you are sinless but you will sin less."

All of This Adds up to Real Change

We have seen there are two drastic differences between what Jesus called a *good fish* and a *bad fish*. One will go on to live in God's presence for an eternity of rejoicing. The other will suffer through that same eternity in a place that is fitting for the punishment of the devil. The stakes are higher than anything else you will ever face, and only you can make the decision that must be made.

We have also seen how important every person is to God and how your heart must be changed in order for your life and eternity to be changed. Then we looked at why Jesus did what He did and why He had to do it the way He did it. Everything had to be done legally. We also looked at how you

---

8   http://www.christianitytoday.com/ct/2013/october-web-only/billy-graham-inter view-my-hope-easy-believism.html

can tell in this life you are ready for the next one. We talked about how God has prepared a way for us to live the way Jesus did with the same power and results that Jesus had by the baptism of the Holy Spirit. Finally, we realized that trying your best or outdoing the next guy in doing good will never transform you into a *good fish*. You must believe in Jesus for this.

It is now time to make that decision. A simple step in the right direction will begin the journey into your new life knowing and following God. The journey is not complete in one step, but it is the starting place. We live each day headed toward our prize of knowing God and experiencing all of the rich and satisfying life He has for us.

What is that first step? For most people it is the prayerful response to hearing the Gospel of what Jesus has done for us. The words are often spoken by a believer and repeated by the one taking that step. The words are important, but the heart is just as important. *You must believe the words you are repeating in order for the transformation from bad fish to good fish to take place.* Today is your day of salvation! Agree with what God wants for you by prayerfully repeating this prayer out loud with all sincerity of heart:

Heavenly Father,
I thank You for loving me so much.
I understand that Jesus came and lived a perfect, sinless life
and although He was innocent, He chose to die in my place
so I could belong to You.
I receive the forgiveness Jesus offers me through His life sacrifice
that was offered to pay for my guilt against You.
I receive your invitation to know You.
Thank You for Your Holy Spirit that I welcome to live in me
and baptize me now in Your power so I can live for you,

boldly speak the truth in love, and confirm the Good News in my life
by Your power that Jesus said would be in me and on me.
Thank You for this new life in You
and for the authority and
freedom to live as Jesus did
and for victory over the devil.

Saying this prayer from the heart is the first step in your new life in Him. You have been born again! Once you were born into Adam's family, but now, through faith in Jesus, you have been born again into the family of God. This is a complete work in the spirit, but a renewing work in the soul and body. Your life of adventure in Him is made up of many steps each day! He is with you, and He will never leave you. The remainder of this book is to help you in your new life, to renew your mind, and learn how to walk.

Chapter Takeaways

1. *Good fish* have a new identity and their new life's focus is to learn who they are in Christ.

2. A *bad fish* relying on good behavior for eternal salvation is deceived and headed to hell.

3. A *good fish* with bad sinful behavior has legally been set free but is practicing a life of slavery to sin again. They can experience their freedom by turning to God and submitting to the Word, which redirects or renew their minds and lifestyle again.

4. It is time to be born again. Put your trust in Jesus instead of yourself and become born again and baptized in the Holy Spirit's power.

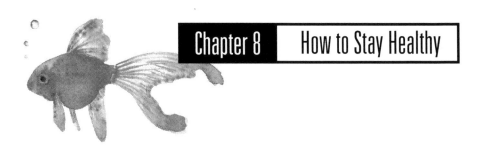

The waters of the world are filled with some amazing fish. There are some fish that look like rocks, there are some fish that have their eyes on one side of their head so they can lay on the bottom of the ocean, there are some fish that hunt in schools and can devour a whole cow in a few minutes.[1] God is a creative God, and His wonders are beautifully displayed underwater.

Perhaps one of the most amazing creatures that swim is the salmon. The salmon start life in freshwater streams and swim towards the ocean as they develop from a small fry into a mature fish. They undergo a chemical change called, "smolting" to help them change from freshwater to saltwater fish and back to a freshwater fish.

This is a rare animal who can begin life in freshwater streams with a salinity closely measured to 0, transform to live life in a salinity that burns at 30 parts per thousand, then return to freshwater again after reversing the process. After having a saltwater aquarium for years, I have seen the effects of slight changes in water quality with fish. These extreme differences would normally burn their protective shield off; painfully killing the fish. Yet God created the salmon to thrive this way. This is why they are sometimes referred to as a "super fish."[2]

---

1   http://www.smithsonianmag.com/science-nature/14-fun-facts-about-piranhas-180951948/?no-ist

2   http://www.streamexplorers.org/fish-facts/salmon-life-cycle

However, there is more to this amazing creature than just that. When their internal homing device goes off, they begin the long swim back to the exact place of their birth. They swim from saltwater to fresh again. They swim upstream and many times jump up waterfalls to get to where they are headed. This trek is a beautiful pilgrimage that leaves the adult fish exhausted, and after laying her eggs she eventually dies. Life is reproduced and comes to an end in the "super fish's" beautiful story.

The salmon reminds me of the *good fish* that exists in one environment, but only as a foreigner. This parallels with the believer's life in 2 Corinthians 5:6: "So we are always confident, even though we know that as long as we live in these bodies we are not at home with the Lord." Similarly, Hebrews 13:14 says, "For this world is not our permanent home; we are looking forward to a home yet to come."

Like the salmon, we are not home and our lives are spent swimming upstream to the prevailing thoughts, values and lifestyles of our current environment. *We know that we are children of God and that the world around us is under the control of the evil one."* (1 John 5:19). *"The thief's purpose is to steal and kill and destroy. My purpose is to give them a rich and satisfying life."* (John 10:10). The *good fish* has God for him but he lives life in a hostile environment that constantly works to keep him from maturing and being fruitful in life. Here are some primary habits or lifestyle choices that can help you to grow and not be vulnerable.

Swim With a Good School

Salmon swim in schools, especially when they are younger, primarily for protection.[3] Jesus told us to go make disciples not converts.[4] Many times believers have shared the Gospel with those who are spiritually blind and eternally lost, urging them to say a quick prayer and give a good confession of faith, and then leaving them to fend for themselves as new believers. I understand this desire to quickly make converts because eternity is at stake. However, our real goal is to make disciples. This takes time, effort, and resources. It is a longer, more deliberate process than repeating a simple prayer. This is why we see healthy, *good fish* swimming in schools—or in good churches where they are intentional about discipleship.

Raising a hand in a church service and walking down the aisle in an altar call may be part of our initial transformation, but it will take submission to the Word of God in order to see lasting change. This takes preaching and teaching or proclaiming and explaining the Word. A good church is an environment of perpetual encouragement, focused on preaching and teaching with understanding and love, that offers opportunities for believers to serve and reach beyond their walls with the Good News.

When a *bad fish* hears the Good News and believes it, a change takes place in his heart and mind. In order for that change to redefine him in all areas of life, he needs to learn what the Word says about living life and submit to God's ways of doing things. This is a radical change for the *bad fish*. It is a complete overhaul of his way of thinking, acting and speaking. Change like this takes a new environment. This is why God has given each *good fish* the church as a great gift.

There is a reason the Bible calls the child of God a "Saint," and it calls His children the "Church." "Saint" is from the Greek word, *hagios,* which means separated and called to God.[5] This is because God has called you out of

---

3   https://www.nps.gov/olym/learn/nature/the-salmon-life-cycle.htm

4   Matthew 28:19

5   Saint - "one separated from the world and consecrated to God" - https://www.blueletterbible.org/search/Dictionary/viewTopic.cfm?topic=ET0003183

the world and into his family. The word for church is *ekklēsia*. It means, "called out" and "assembly."[6] The church is God's plan to reach the world and encourage the believer in following Jesus as a disciple. We cannot overstate the magnitude of transformation that begins when the *bad fish* hears and accepts God's Gospel. It is more than a paradigm shift of thinking, which is why Jesus called it being "born again."[7] God, in His wisdom and love, has prepared a family for baby Christians to protect and provide the nourishment they need to grow up and mature out of vulnerability.

The simple truth is a good church will help you to grow exponentially faster than floundering through your days alone, isolated from His family in a world that is hostile to the child of God. Those who make a decision, after hearing the Gospel to follow Christ but go right back to the spiritually cold hardened world and filth, will find change harder than those who commit to go and grow with a Bible believing, Spirit-filled local church.

John Maxwell points out in his book *The 15 Invaluable Laws of Growth*, "If you try to... Change yourself but not your environment—growth will be slow and difficult; Change your environment but not yourself—growth will be slow and less difficult; Change your environment and yourself—growth will be faster and more successful. By putting both together at the same time, you increase and accelerate your chances for success."[8] This is firm reality about growth and change.

---

6   Church – "ekklēsia: an assembly of Christians gathered for worship in a religious meeting" https://www.blueletterbible.org/lang/lexicon/lexicon.cfm?ot=NASB& strongs=G1577&t=KJV#lexSearch

7   Born Again - See John 3:3-8

8   Maxwell, John (2012). *The 15 Invaluable Laws of Growth: Live Them and Reach Your Potential* [E-book]. New York, New York: Center Street Hachette Book Group

A good church will be committed to a healthy environment where worship is not defined as merely a musical presentation, but as an engagement of the heart, fueling the desire to be a living sacrifice in spirit and truth for His glory.[9] It is a place where community operates in the fruitfulness of diversity in concert with the beauty of unity. God makes His children one so the world may see this and believe.[10] Finally, the church is where believers serve one another using the practical and spiritual gifts as the Holy Spirit disperses.[11] Discipleship flourishes in this unified environment as believers mature into the fullness of Christ as He designed us to do.

Sadly, not every local church was healthy in the New Testament. This is still an issue today as the late Reverend Billy Graham points out: "Many churches of all persuasions are hiring research agencies to poll neighborhoods, asking what kind of church they prefer; then the local churches design themselves to fit the desires of the people. True faith in God that demands selflessness is being replaced by trendy religion that serves the selfish."[12]

Church doctrine or the message must be based on the Word of God, not experience or trendy viewpoints. As noted above, being a part of a good church will help you exponentially to grow in renewing your mind. However, sometimes churches put their doctrine above the Word. If it is in the Word, and supported by the context of at least two or three verses and it is New Covenant then you should put your faith in it to receive it and expect it to be part of your life experience.

---

9   Romans 12:1-2; John 4:23-24

10   John 17:20-21

11   Billy Graham - http://www.huffingtonpost.com/2013/10/06/billy-graham-book-the-reason-for-my-hope-salvation_n_4025835.html

12   Colossians 2:15

The truth supersedes any denomination's rich history or what the community believes. If what is taught is contrary to the Word, it is not the truth. If the message does not embrace the whole truth or attempts to explain away the promises of God's Word, reject it. Sometimes people base what they believe on experience, rather than the truth of God's Word. Can you imagine if Peter, a fisherman by *experience*, would have done that *instead of listening to Jesus* to get out of the boat and walk on the water? If a local church does not teach the Good News of Jesus and our response to what He has accomplished, the Lordship of Jesus, or your identity in Christ concerning you can have, do or be what the Word says, you may need to look for a school of *good fish* that are committed to the Word.

The devil has two black eyes and was beaten soundly, but he will not quit. He knows his time is short. His only power today is deception. Sin and death were dealt with on the cross of Jesus. So the devil has been disarmed.[13] As the Good News is preached, his captives are now released, the blind see, the oppressed are set free, and we can all run headlong into this time of the Lord's favor.[14]

The enemy's job is impossible, but he is somehow still deceiving *bad fish* into staying *bad fish*, *bad fish* into thinking they are *good fish*, and *good fish* into thinking they are still *bad fish*. When you believe what the devil has said over what God has said, you're following in Adam's footsteps instead of Jesus' guidance.

---

13   Luke 4:18-19
14   https://www.blueletterbible.org/lang/lexicon/lexicon.cfm?Strongs=G281&t=KJV

Daily Bread – The Word Of God

A *good fish* is a follower of Christ. He takes the word and lives by it. As he reads it and meditates on it, praying for revelation, the internal witness that is in our hearts says, "Amen!—God this is so!" The word, "amen," actually means, "God make it so" or "may it be fulfilled."[15] Under the New Covenant, we can say it with faith and strong affirmation as in, "God, I agree this is in my heart and life... right now!"

The Bible is an external book written on paper, bound by leather. But the *good fish* is not only armed with Word of God in his hands, but it is also is written on his heart, written on his spirit, and bound by the blood of Jesus.[16] The process of growing as a *good fish* takes place every time you prayerfully read the external Word. It comes to the heart through the mind. As it reaches the heart, it sparks new revelation and understanding rises. The Spirit is now able to convict or convince the mind to believe the Word in a deeper, convicted way with supernatural faith.

When you give your heart to Jesus, your heart is changed. However, the Bible says your mind must be renewed.[17] Prayerfully reading God's Bible is the process of faith that will transform your mind from *bad fish* into *good fish* thinking. You have a crucial part in God's process to live in Him and for Him. Many believers do not read their Bible, and that is why they are ignorant and drifting in paralyzed unbelief, floating downstream. They do not know who they are, what they have been given, or what they are called to do.

---

15   Jeremiah 31:33; Hebrews 8:10 and 10:16
16   Romans 12:2; Ephesians 4:22-24
17   James 3:4

Instead of facing each day as a *good fish* with the Kingdom of God's agenda, they brace for each day, trying to survive until Jesus comes. A believer should not go through life white-knuckled, afraid of what the day will bring, waiting for the other shoe to drop! The Word tells them to live with the hope for eternity, but they exist in a life of fear and fail to impact the world because they do not read it regularly.

Guard Your Heart

There are some *good fish* that became *good fish* twenty years ago but never matured; their growth stunted. Like the Israelites who, after leaving the bondage of Egypt, wandered around in the wilderness for forty years and then died without inheriting the Promised Land, they they've made no progress in the Kingdom of God.

Some churches are full of believers who feed on the old way of living, the world's opinion, or the devil's lies. When a believer feeds on the same things as the lost world, he will get the same results. They are the target audience for those commercials on Christian radio stations where sickness, anxiety and depression are still creating issues for them. They have never learned that what you sow into your heart will eventually become a harvest.

Proverbs 4:23 admonishes us to, "Guard your heart above all else, for it determines the course of your life." Your life is determined by what your heart chooses to believe. Your heart chooses what to believe from the options you expose it to. When we leave the gates of our heart open and abandon our guard post, we eventually become hardened to the direction and passion for the things of God. Today, many *good fish* are cynical and have become so hardened they cannot believe God for His promises. This tragedy leaves their lives looking and smelling like the *bad fish*. They are

> Your heart chooses what to believe from the options you expose it to.

wandering in the desert instead of walking in God's promises by faith. Their testimony is, "God did something in my life years ago... but not much has happened lately."

This is our own fault. Jesus said, "Wherever your treasure is, there the desires of your heart will also be." (Matthew 6:21 and Luke 12:34). This means whatever you treasure, set your heart on, or value in life will become your heart's desire. God is not free to move in their lives because He is ignored. This produces the same life results as the *bad fish* that is completely ignorant of Him. This kind of life does not give a good testimony of God's salvation in the *good fish's* life to the *bad fish* watching him.

A hardened heart will stifle the move of God in your life. Jesus rebuked the disciples after they had experienced some great miracles because they still had hard unbelieving hearts: *"Jesus knew what they were saying, so he said, 'Why are you arguing about having no bread? Don't you know or understand even yet? Are your hearts too hard to take it in? 'You have eyes—can't you see? You have ears—can't you hear?' Don't you remember anything at all?"* (Mark 8:17-18).

Notice, Jesus pointed out that a symptom of a hardened heart is that it does not "remember anything at all." The disciples did not take time to treasure or consider the wonderful things Jesus had done by praising God or giving thanks. Guarding your heart is both an act of offense and defense. It means you value the right things, and you protect your heart from exposure to the wrong things as much as possible. It is a key toward an increase of receiving more of the life God has prepared for you.

Whatever comes into your eyes and ears will determine your focus and will write an understanding or persuasion on your heart. This is why it is important to watch over your heart by guarding what you intentionally view or listen to in order to gain knowledge. Equally important is guarding what you passively watch and listen to for entertainment.

The *good fish* is called a child of God. We are to be like children, innocent of evil. This is why I am both grieved and appalled when I hear of selfish, lazy parenting that exposes kids to movies or entertainment that streams the world, the flesh and the devil in digital surround sound. Sadly these parents are hardened themselves, stunted in their tenderness toward God, and are hardening their children in these same dull, ineffective, powerless ways. Their kids will have unnecessary hurdles at a young age instead of running headlong into what God has for them.

As an adult, only you can guard your own heart. When you make a choice to protect your innocence and feed on Who He says He is and what He has said about you, your heart will be hardened toward distractions and tender towards His leading. This is a great key to being a healthy *good fish* and being led into a rich and satisfying life of impact.

The Words Of Your Mouth

The words of our mouth are given to us for more than communication. When you speak in agreement with what God's Word says about you, your words become the next step in transforming your mind. God created the world using faith filled words. The Bible teaches us our words have power in them. "Death and life are in the power of the tongue, and those who love it *and* indulge it will eat its fruit *and* bear the consequences of their words." (Proverbs 18:21AMP). When we use our words flippantly to describe our difficult circumstances or the worst-case scenario, our heart gets a picture and starts to put faith into action toward those negative words. The *good fish* who understands this simple, powerful tool will avoid self-defeat and will inject God's power into their circumstances.

We can also acknowledge the devil, trouble or temptations with our words. When we do, we amplify those influences. When you speak about how the devil is beating you up, it is the power of praise in reverse. This is talking yourself into magnifying the enemy instead of how great your God is. You can only expect more of the same attacks to begin to consume your thoughts and life when you tear yourself down by glorifying the devil, trouble or temptations.

Instead, God has encouraged us to acknowledge everything we have been given in Christ instead! "...[T]hat the sharing of your faith may become effective by the acknowledgment of every good thing which is in you in Christ Jesus." (Philemon 6 NKJV). This is how successful, confident people speak. They do not dwell and meditate on or describe the darkness they are facing; they tell their situation about their God.

Remember the story of David and Goliath? David heard the words of Goliath and asked, "Who is this uncircumcised Philistine that he should defy the armies of the living God?" (1 Sam 17:26b NKJV). David became righteously angry, and voiced his faith against the giant while everyone else was trembling. He invoked His covenant with God and reminded everyone that Goliath did not have a covenant. David's words were full of faith in the face of battle. Later in his life, he encouraged himself when everyone else was speaking of stoning him: "And David was greatly distressed; for the people spake of stoning him, because the soul of all the people was grieved, every man for his sons and for his daughters: but David encouraged himself in the Lord his God." (1 Samuel 30:6 KJV).

David became King of Israel and was an ancestor to the Messiah. Part of the reason for his success was his habit of speaking in agreement with God and trusting God in the face of life's dire situations. Just before he launched into a ferocious charge towards Goliath to put an end to his blaspheme against God, he shouted these famous faith-filled words:

> Then David said to the Philistine, "You come to me with a sword, with a spear, and with a javelin. But I come to you in the name of the LORD of hosts, the God of the armies of Israel, whom you have defied. This day the LORD will deliver you into my hand, and I will strike you and take your head from you. And this day I will give the carcasses of the camp of the Philistines to the birds of the air and the wild beasts of the earth, that all the earth may know that there is a God in Israel. Then all this assembly shall know that the LORD does not save with sword and spear; for the battle *is* the LORD's, and He will give you into our hands. (1 Samuel 17:45-47).

David triumphed over the enemy that day and throughout life because he used his words to agree with God and to speak trust instead of fear. He wrote a beautiful prayer in the Psalms, revealing his awareness that He needed God's help even to speak right: *"May the words of my mouth and the meditation of my heart be pleasing to you, O Lord, my rock and my redeemer."* (Psalm 19:14). *"Set a guard over my mouth, Lord; keep watch over the door of my lips."* (Psalm 141:3 NIV).

Jesus showed us how we could speak faith-filled words with sincerity to encourage and bring change in our lives: "A good person produces good things from the treasury of a good heart, and an evil person produces evil things from the treasury of an evil heart. What you say flows from what is in your heart." (Luke 6:45). Similarly, the book of James tells us the tongue is like the small rudder of a great ship. Although it is small, unseen and forgotten by many on board, it is what ultimately steers the majestic vessel.[18]

Our words are used to order pizza, complain about the irritating driver in front of us and shout praises to God on a Sunday morning during the worship hour. Healthy *good fish* realize the importance of our words. They avoid the three C's: criticizing, complaining or condemning. They speak in agreement with what God's Word has said about them. This is a simple, extraordinary way to transform your mind and use your words to live a life that gives God glory.

Prayer and Praise

Prayer and praise are other wonderful ways God uses to transform our minds and build our faith into believing Him for overcoming-victory. *'For every child of God defeats this evil world, and we achieve this victory through our faith."* (1 John 5:4). The devil knows this and knew he needed to deceive the church into prayer that is void of revelation and full of unbelief. He had an impossible task. However, we have seen that he knows how to deceive.

Is it possible to pray wrongly? Absolutely. Prayer is not simply sharing your heart with the Lord or complaining to God about your circumstances. If you want to pray with results it will always take faith. If you want your faith enacted toward the correct thing it will always take a working knowledge of the Word. Remember the Word reveals what Jesus gave us, who we are in Him and what we have been empowered to do through Christ. ***"When you pray, don't be like the hypocrites who love to pray*** *publicly on street corners*

---

18   Jude 20-21, Romans 8:26-27; 1 Corinthians 14:17; Isaiah 28:11-12 (NKJV)

and in the synagogues where everyone can see them. I tell you the truth, that is all the reward they will ever get." (Emphasis mine) (Matthew 6:5).

Jesus said, "hypocrites... love to pray." We do not pray in order to look spiritual or to act godly; we pray because we *are* spiritual, and we *are* godly. Prayer is voicing our hearts of faith in Him and seeking God's intervention in our circumstances to line up with God's Word.

Praying in tongues, as our Flying Fish does, is the supernatural way to build your faith and keep yourself in the love of God no matter how bad the circumstances are around you. It is also the way to pray when you do not know how to pray about something. His Holy Spirit will lead you into voicing His perfect will using your tongue. Although you do not understand in your mind you can trust He is saying what needs to be said in order to get done what needs to be done. This is a way to become peaceful in the face of trying confusing situations.[19]

Prayer with understanding takes focus. Praise helps us to bring our hearts and minds into correct focus no matter what we are facing. There are many times in the scripture when the people praised God for Who He is, and because of His promise before the physical manifestation of a breakthrough. King Jehoshaphat's story in 2 Chronicles 20 is a perfect example of this. There were three kings from the surrounding nations who rose up against him and the people of Judah. The only reasonable outcome was his complete defeat. However, he cried out to God for His help, reminding God and himself that they were God's chosen children. *"And now see what the armies of Ammon, Moab, and Mount Seir are doing. ...O our God, won't you stop them? We are powerless against this mighty army that is about to*

---

19   http://www.livescience.com/56047-why-is-dead-sea-so-salty.html

attack us. We do not know what to do, but we are looking to you for help." (2 Chronicles 20:10-12).

God's spirit came upon a young man from among the people as they sought God. He gave a "Word," a message, inspired by the Holy Spirit to the people that God would fight this battle! They all praised God for this "Word" of encouragement.

> *He said, "Listen, all you people of Judah and Jerusalem! Listen, King Jehoshaphat! This is what the Lord says: Do not be afraid! Don't be discouraged by this mighty army, for the battle is not yours, but God's. Tomorrow, march out against them. ...you will not even need to fight. Take your positions; then stand still and watch the Lord's victory. He is with you, O people of Judah and Jerusalem. Do not be afraid or discouraged. Go out against them tomorrow, for the Lord is with you!"*

> *Then King Jehoshaphat bowed low with his face to the ground. And all the people of Judah and Jerusalem did the same, worshiping the Lord. Then the Levites from the clans of Kohath and Korah stood to praise the Lord, the God of Israel, with a very loud shout.* (2 Chronicles 20:15-19).

The next day was the day of battle. Because the people had slept since the Word was given, Jehoshaphat reminded them of what God had said. Then the people agreed to march towards the battle armed with faith in God in their hearts. This faith was heard as the praise team was placed at the front of the army. "...the king appointed singers to walk ahead of the army, singing to the Lord and praising him for his holy splendor. This is what they sang: "Give thanks to the Lord; his faithful love endures forever!" (2 Chronicles 20:21). The people began to praise God singing, "Praise the Lord, His love endures forever!"

We should take note, they were not singing "Praise the Lord we are going to crush our enemy." Their focus was correct. They were not *thinking* about the enemy or the real battle that faced them over the hill. They were not *thinking* about their strategy of warfare. The circumstances were grim, but they were *focused* on their God and did not have double vision.

Meanwhile, on the other side of the hill:

> At the very moment they began to sing and give praise, the Lord caused the armies of Ammon, Moab, and Mount Seir to start fighting among themselves. The armies of Moab and Ammon turned against their allies from Mount Seir and killed every one of them. After they had destroyed the army of Seir, they began attacking each other. So when the army of Judah arrived at the lookout point in the wilderness, all they saw were dead bodies lying on the ground as far as they could see. Not a single one of the enemies had escaped.

> King Jehoshaphat and his men went out to gather the plunder. They found vast amounts of equipment, clothing, and other valuables—more than they could carry. There was so much plunder that it took them three days just to collect it all! On the fourth day they gathered in the Valley of Blessing, which got its name that day because the people praised and thanked the Lord there. It is still called the Valley of Blessing today. (2 Chronicles 20:22-26).

What are you facing today? The odds were overwhelmingly stacked against Jehoshaphat and the people of Judah. Some would have prayed all day and then spent the day riddled with unbelief knowing God *could*, but wondering if He *would*. Prayer and praise work together to ask God and then believe God no matter what the circumstances are telling you. When you pray, spend some time praising God for Who He is. "His love endures forever!" Fear cannot survive in this type of sincere praise environment. *"There is no fear in love. On the contrary, love that has achieved its goal gets rid of fear, because fear has to do with punishment; the person who keeps fearing has not been brought to maturity in regard to love."* 1 John 4:18 (CJB).

Praising God will bring focus to life and stir your heart to believe with renewed strength. Praising God will remove your focus off of your problems and put it on your source and solution! Praising God will make you aware of God in your life situations. Praising God for Who He is and His love for you will convince you that you are loved and will drive out all fear.

Look Outside of Yourself

The Dead Sea has streams and underwater springs flowing into it but there is not an outlet.[20] "This inland body of water is appropriately named because its high mineral content allows nothing to live in its waters."[21] It was called "The Devil's Sea" at one time. Its shoreline is actually the lowest point on earth for dry land at "1300 feet below sea level."[22] The Dead Sea is a perfect metaphor for the unhealthy *good fish* who lives each day receiving, but never gives.

---

20 http://www.bibleplaces.com/deadsea/
21 http://www.bibleplaces.com/deadsea/
22 John 8:44 especially in the NIV

Jesus told us we were to be a city on a hill and a lamp that should not be hidden. The purpose of a lamp is to give light. Today, a purpose of the church is to be the light of the world. A healthy *good fish* is someone who receives God's truth and shares what he knows with other believers for encouragement and with the lost in the world around him. This is so that they can respond and come to know God.

God gave us the picture of health every time you inhale and exhale. If you only received oxygen, your body would die. We are built to receive and to give. Some *good fish* are unhealthy because they refuse to give. They are hiding from the world and life has become a waiting game of survival until the rapture. We are meant for so much more. The more you receive of God's Word, the more your heart should be compelled to give.

The love of God is lavishly given to us partly because it is meant to overflow onto others. Paul told us His kindness leads to repentance. Loving others not only identifies us as believers, it is the action that causes us to grow. The Apostle John tells us when we love others whom we can see, God's love is perfected in us. *"And as we live in God, our love grows more perfect..."* (1 John 4:17a).

A healthy *good fish* is one who is concerned with those around him and beyond him. Jesus knew the Father loved Him, yet He was filled with compassion for the hurting and the lost in the world. When you know God, you are compelled to share His heart for others. *"Dear friends, let us continue to love one another, for love comes from God. Anyone who loves is a child of God and knows God. But anyone who does not love does not know God, for God is love."* (1 John 4:7-8).

We love others in simple ways, like determining to be a positive voice at work, by smiling and encouraging others. Love can be tangible such as giving a cup of cold water to the thirsty or taking time to help someone in need. Serving, tithing, giving to missions, and working enthusiastically toward the vision of the church are ways to give and grow. One of the greatest ways you can love is by speaking the truth in compassion by sharing the Good News of what Jesus has done for you with someone. These are ways to be healthy and live free from a self-absorbed, stunted, unhealthy life.

Many years ago while I was praying for our church's impact in our county, I heard these words in my spirit, "Erase the distaste and change the native language." Although these were somewhat peculiar words, I immediately understood them. Our church was to raise a banner of righteousness and ethical behavior that would be respectable, while serving the people in benevolent meaningful ways. We would not just preach the Good News with our words, we would live it with our lives.

Jesus told the religious people who looked good on the outside but did not know Him in their hearts that lying was their *native language*.[23] This is true of our time. We are surrounded by compromise and a constant bending of the truth to manage perspective. It is not hard to shine when things are so dark.

The other day I was checking out at the cashier's desk at an automotive dealer. We had some warranty work done, but agreed to pay one hundred dollars toward it. They forgot to bill us, and I asked about it. They went into overdrive to see if I was right. When they confirmed this to be true, they thanked me and with stunned gratitude said, "You are an honest man. We don't see that very often." This is a real problem. In order to change the

---

23   John 17:3

native language, hearts have to change. Love is the way to open a heart. A life of love is made up of decisions to be ethical and uncompromising, considering what is best not only for ourselves but for others.

A *good fish* lives to know God and give Him glory. Today, the church holds events, meetings, conferences and rallies to bring the *bad fish* to hear the Gospel and become *good fish*. However, when you live as a child of the light, everyday opportunities, like shopping at Wal-Mart become transformative ones. The surprising beauty is that this kind of living helps the *bad fish* come to know Jesus and the *good fish* to be healthy. Life grows in us when we lift our heads and minister in the everyday world around us. This is a necessity in staying healthy as a *good fish*.

Make a commitment to change your environment to support your decisions as much as possible by primarily becoming a part of the school of *good fish*—a good church. Renew your mind by prayerfully reading God's Word daily. Speak in agreement with God. Pray with faith in God's Word and praise God for Who He is. Finally, live to give. A believer who only receives is stunted in their growth. Giving and serving are ways you love. As you exercise love, it grows. These simple healthy habits will help you to grow quickly in knowing Him.

Chapter Takeaways

1. *Good fish* have habits that help them to transform their mind.
2. A *good fish* goes to a good local church; loves and lives by the Word; guards his heart; is watchful about how he speaks; actively prays; praises God through life; and lives to give.

"Wal-Mart is a great fishing spot"

— *Meme*

I recently met a *good fish* who is the grandmother of a young lady in our youth group. They call her Meme. She is an unassuming, precious little lady who makes darkness tremble when she prays these simple words each day, "Holy Spirit, I make myself available to you today."

These words have transformed even a simple trip to Wal-Mart into a Holy Spirit fishing excursion. She has told me story after story about feeling led to by the Holy Spirit to start up a conversation with complete strangers she meets. She does not naturally like to talk to unknown people but the awkwardness of meeting a tall, imposing male individual is quickly forgotten after a few moments of small talk used by the Holy Ghost. Many of the people in her encounters have tearfully asked for prayer because they had just been diagnosed with cancer or some other influence of terror. The Holy Ghost knew these people were hurting and sent a *good fish* to find them and minister to them.

Bad fish have met Jesus at Wal-Mart because Meme invited the Lord to lead her and she was willing to follow. God will use the simplest things in this world to confound the wise. He will send a simple fisherman to share with the lost the story of the cross, which legally purchased their freedom and tell them about the hope He has for them to now come into His family.

Jesus is a fisherman and always knows where the fish are. When he was choosing the men who would follow him and eventually carry on His ministry of reconciling[1] the people to God, he decided upon some men who fished for a living. There is a wealth of understanding to learn about reaching others with the message of life from the parallel of how to catch fish. In three out of the four Gospels, Jesus invited His disciples to follow Him and fish for the lost: "Jesus called out to them, 'Come, follow me, and I will show you how to fish for people!'" (Matthew 4:19 and Mark 1:17). See also Luke 5:1-11,

> One day as Jesus was preaching on the shore of the Sea of Galilee, great crowds pressed in on him to listen to the word of God. He noticed two empty boats at the water's edge, for the fishermen had left them and were washing their nets. Stepping into one of the boats, Jesus asked Simon, its owner, to push it out into the water. So he sat in the boat and taught the crowds from there. When he had finished speaking, he said to Simon, "Now go out where it is deeper, and let down your nets to catch some fish." "Master," Simon replied, "we worked hard all last night and didn't catch a thing. But if you say so, I'll let the nets down again." And this time their nets were so full of fish they began to tear! A shout for help brought their partners in the other boat, and soon both boats were filled with fish and on the verge of sinking.

> When Simon Peter realized what had happened, he fell to his knees before Jesus and said, "Oh, Lord, please leave

---

1   2 Corinthians 5:19-20

me—I'm such a sinful man." For he was awestruck by the number of fish they had caught, as were the others with him. His partners, James and John, the sons of Zebedee, were also amazed.

Jesus replied to Simon, "Don't be afraid! From now on you'll be fishing for people!" And as soon as they landed, they left everything and followed Jesus.

A Good Fish Is Also a Good Fisherman

When you gave your heart to Jesus you were not immediately raptured out of here and ushered into the presence of the Father in glory. Instead, glory set up shop in you and began to transform you into an agent of change in this fallen world. He saved you, and He wants everyone to come to repentance and enter into life. Once we respond to Him, He empowers us, and He sends us back into the world as new creations to bring others to Him.

Remember, this world is lost and still under the influence of the devil.[2] The way people come to life is by hearing, accepting and believing the Good News about Jesus. Legally neither the devil nor God can go against your will and force you to follow them. We must agree with one or the other that there is no middle ground. Agreeing with God is called, "Faith."

As we've stated before, all men are guilty until they accept the forgiveness of God, and they enter into life by accepting Jesus' offer of a place in God's family. That means everyone is lost until they believe and receive Christ as

---

2   Ephesians 2:2-3; 1 John 5:19

their Savior and Lord. This requires repentance. Repentance is the sign of a spiritual awakening in your life and in a society.

It's important to review again here what repentance really is. The New Testament of the Bible was written in Greek. The Greek word for repentance is "metanoia," which means to reverse your belief and act differently.[3] Many think it is just feeling sorry about the bad things you have done. Although the sorrow of regret is usually part of true repentance, there is also an overwhelming sense of relief and joy when you realize the error of your thinking and change to the mind of Christ—leading to a rich and satisfying life that brings Him glory. This is why repentance is always part of the process when a person hears the Good News and accepts it.

A *good fish* shares this Good News as naturally as a generous man shares his meal with a starving man. *There is a sense of urgency, excitement, compassion and righteous purpose beating in the heart of the believer.* It is the work of the Holy Spirit in our lives. He is leading into God's plan and feeding new desires to live a life pleasing to the Father.[4] The devil works through the influence of the world, the flesh and with spiritual opposition to quench these desires.

A *good fish* is living from a new heart, which produces a new life where Jesus is Lord. Jesus said it like this: *"A good person produces good things from the treasury of a good heart, and an evil person produces evil things from the treasury of an evil heart. What you say flows from what is in your heart."* (Luke 6:45).

---

3   https://www.blueletterbible.org/lang/Lexicon/Lexicon.cfm?strongs=G3341&t=KJV
4   Romans 8:14; Philippians 2:13

> *A good fish shares this Good News as naturally as a generous man shares his meal with a starving man.*

After the resurrection Jesus was going to ascend to the Father. He and the disciples met at a mountain, and He gave them the Great Commission to, *"...go and make disciples of all the nations, baptizing them in the name of the Father and the Son and the Holy Spirit. Teach these new disciples to obey all the commands I have given you. And be sure of this: I am with you always, even to the end of the age."* (Matthew 28:19-20).

We see in the book of Acts, He told them to wait in Jerusalem for the Holy Spirit to come upon and empower them to do what He commanded. A *good fish* naturally and actively works at the Great Commission because his heart beats to share the Good News. Jesus is the Lord of his life and He is empowered by the Holy Spirit to confirm His message is true. "Go into all the world' means God wants you to go into all of your world and share the gospel." — Greg Laurie[5]

Only You Can Be You For Him

The other day my wife and I were visiting with an art teacher from our area who, as we were visiting, trailed off and stopped talking in mid-sentence. She felt compelled to say that I was the long lost twin brother to her uncle. She said that my personality, mannerisms, and build were so similar that it was uncanny. I awkwardly laughed it off until she showed

---

5   Harvest America@HarvestAmerica Sep 29 6:10 pm via Twitter

me his picture. It was a bit odd and gave us all a good laugh seeing we were so similar in appearance.

No matter how closely you resemble someone, however, you are still an absolute original. When God made you in His image, He did not make another. God has created you unlike any other person that has ever lived on the planet. When He created you, He called you into His Kingdom and service. God gave you skills and many of the desires you have at birth. However, they have to be cultivated and developed. Coach Jay Carty says: "I believe the Bible teaches that each of us has been given the potential to make a significant contribution to God's kingdom. This contribution comes about when we apply our skills and gifts. The potential to be skillful is given at physical birth, and spiritual gifts are given at the time of spiritual birth. Both skills and gifts must be discovered and developed."[6]

People usually go into a certain occupation to provide for their families based on their God given desires, skills or inclinations. The darkened world will try to influence and twist these things to distort the original purpose. Part of developing them for God's glory is to keep your mind renewed through meditation in His Word and fellowship with Him. When you live to give God glory He can take an ordinary shepherd's staff and use it in your hands to deliver a nation. He can take a sack lunch and feed multitudes of hungry people. He can use your love for fishing and use it to rescue those who are headed for a devil's eternal torment and bring them into a life of knowing God. It is not by accident that Jesus took men who were doing something they did to make a living and transformed it into a way to help others come to life.

---

6   Wooden, John R. *Coach Wooden's Pyramid of Success*. Ventura, California: Regal Books from Gospel Light, 2005. Pg 76

Today, we think of ministry in compartments. Somehow it has become a profession for the few instead of part of the identity of a *good fish*. We have subtly allowed the message that living life for Jesus is private and separate from making a living. The truth is, only you can be you for Him. When you live for Him, He will make a difference in the lives of others through you, even on a simple trip to Wal-Mart. When you say, "Holy Spirit I am available for you today," you are breaking out of that Christian box the world tries to put in. He wants who you are and what you do for a living to be an influence in making a difference in the Kingdom of God. When your living this way, you will be bringing others to Him, encouraging those who are already His, and seeing your own life be fruitful, purposeful and victorious!

> The truth is, only you can be you for Him.

Making a Living Can Be Making a Life

There is a teaching that breaks down winning our world for Him known as, "The Seven Cultural Mountains."[7] These are seven separate areas identified in our society where the battle is raging for the hearts of men and their eternities. Wherever the church brings a strong influence for the Kingdom of God with the message of reconciliation to Him, the believers prosper and the harvest is great for life. However, when the church retreats or loses ground in these areas, the world slips into darkness and confusion, leading to destruction today and for eternity.

The seven areas are identified as: business/commerce, media, government, education, family, arts and entertainment/sports, and the church.

---

7   http://www.7culturalmountains.org/

While there are subgroups to each of these, what you do for a living may be placed in one of these categories. The basic point is this ministry for the *good fish* is in whatever you do because you do it for God's glory. When you live like this you will find yourself not only prosperous and encouraging, but also a fisher of people.

The Definition Of Success

Jesus was the most accomplished and successful man who ever lived. He lived only to do the will of His Father with every breath. He was in constant communion with Him as He walked this planet in the flesh. He said: *"I tell you the truth, the Son can do nothing by himself. He does only what he sees the Father doing. Whatever the Father does, the Son also does. For the Father loves the Son and shows him everything he is doing. In fact, the Father will show him how to do even greater works than healing this man. Then you will truly be astonished."* (John 5:19b-20).

Everything Jesus said, did and where he went was in agreement with Father God. On the night before He went to the cross He prayed these beautiful words: "I brought glory to you here on earth by completing the work you gave me to do." (John 17:4). In this sentence Jesus recalibrated the definition of success for us.

In another parable, Jesus taught about being faithful stewards with what we have been given. Two of the stewards were given similar praise for using what they were given to be used for God's glory: *"The master was full of praise. 'Well done, my good and faithful servant. You have been faithful in handling this small amount, so now I will give you many more respon-sibilities. Let's celebrate together!'"* (Matthew 25:21). But to the one who neglected and hid his gifts, He declared:

"But the master replied, 'You wicked and lazy servant! If you knew I harvested crops I didn't plant and gathered crops I didn't cultivate, why didn't you deposit my money in the bank? At least I could have gotten some interest on it.'

"Then he ordered, 'Take the money from this servant, and give it to the one with the ten bags of silver. To those who use well what they are given, even more will be given, and they will have an abundance. But from those who do nothing, even what little they have will be taken away. Now throw this useless servant into outer darkness, where there will be weeping and gnashing of teeth.' (Matthew 25:26-30).

As a child of God we live life to the fullest with purpose bringing people to Him:

The Apostle Paul points this out: *"Through Christ, God has given us the privilege and authority as apostles to tell Gentiles everywhere what God has done for them, so that they will believe and obey him, bringing glory to his name."* (Romans 1:5).

As a *good fish*, you have a position in His family; you have a purpose to do good works that He planned for you to do long ago. These good works help you to live a healthy, meaningful life that brings glory to God. They empower you to rescue those who are still in the lost and destructive life you were once in. In short, every day with Jesus can be a miraculous one that brings you higher in life and affect all of eternity for the Kingdom of God!

When we yield, like Meme does on her way to Wal-Mart, this decision allows simple things to transform the world around us. We are *good fish* living the good life. The Apostle Peter agrees: *"Do you have the gift of speaking? Then speak as though God himself were speaking through you. Do you have the gift of helping others? Do it with all the strength and energy that God supplies. Then everything you do will bring glory to God through Jesus Christ. All glory and power to him forever and ever! Amen."* (1 Peter 4:11).

Just Keep Swimming

The *good fish's* good life is not always easy but it is always life. When you live out of your relationship with Jesus, you are abiding in Him. He is the author of life, and He will infuse you with life as you walk with Him through ordinary days no matter what challenges lie in front of you.

Once again, in the movie *Finding Nemo*,[8] Nemo's father Marlin is discouraged by the hardship of the journey. Then his traveling companion, Dory, begins to sing a simple, repetitive song—"Just Keep Swimming." When life seems impossible, becomes exceptionally difficult or passes through the valley of grief, just keep swimming. Marlin had a mission. He could not give up. His purpose was to seek and save that which was lost. He knew there would be so much joy when he found his son!

Today, there is work to be done, but also a rest that we enter into. When you become a child of God He calls you into His service. You rest from your own self-dependence and trust Him for success in what you set your hand to. He will make your work prosper. You can do great things even on a trip to Wal-Mart, actually "greater things" than you have ever imagined. When we pursue God's plan for us instead of our own agenda, we can rest knowing He will equip us to do it and make us fruitful for His glory. One of

---

8   http://www.imdb.com/title/tt0266543/trivia?tab=qt&ref_=tt_trv_qu

the most beautiful prayers in the Bible is: *"May he equip you with all you need for doing his will. May he produce in you, through the power of Jesus Christ, every good thing that is pleasing to him. All glory to him forever and ever! Amen."* (Hebrews 13:21).

Good Only Gets Better!

There are two types of fish in Jesus' parable; both have an eternal destination. The decision to accept Jesus' free gift of life now determines not only your quality and purpose in this life, but more importantly, your eternal life. We have seen the process that the Holy Spirit goes through to fish for people in order to redeem them. He values every one of us. We are all considered VIFs. You are more important to Father God's heart than you can comprehend. He desires to see you saved, living passionately with His purpose, filled with His Spirit, growing up into a healthy person with the knowledge of what it means to be a new creation, and having fun.

As a *good fish*, God desires you to grow up and mature in this new life. Maturity means you can be fruitful, yet not easily deceived or vulnerable to the enemy's snares. We now realize even though a person chooses to follow God and pursues living life for Him, the devil works to derail them into a life that is wasted and does not make a difference in the Kingdom of God or the lives of others. The challenge is not to pass time until you enter into glory, but to renew your mind and to stay true to the course.

A *good fish* continues to live the good life through fellowship with the believers, meditating in the Word, guarding his heart, letting his words be influences for God, focusing on Him through praise and prayer, and living to impact others with the life God is producing in him. Jesus said, *"And this is the way to have eternal life—to know you, the only true God, and Jesus*

Christ, the one you sent to earth." (John 17:3). Eternal life does not start when you die and walk through the doorway of death in this life to come face to face with Jesus. This life begins when you say, "Yes," to Jesus' offer for transformation into a *good fish* from a *bad fish*. This new life is a whole new way of living that must be learned and lived by faith in Him.

Remember: We are born to do great things, but born again to do even greater things. Accepting Him and learning to pray, "Holy Spirit I am available to you today," makes life a generous and gracious adventure that changes lives wherever you go. Today is a day unlike any other. The sunrise is full of hope because: *"...we know that God causes everything to work together for the good of those who love God and are called according to his purpose for them."* (Romans 8:28).

So as you swim into the deep blue of each day giving God glory, my hope is that you would take this book and help someone else find new life as a good fish. Together we can see this world transformed one heart at a time into good fish experiencing eternal life, living a fulfilled life, and saved from a wasted life.

Today is your day of salvation! Agree with what God wants for you by prayerfully repeating this prayer out loud with all sincerity of heart:

Heavenly Father,
I thank You for loving me so much.
I understand that Jesus came and lived a perfect, sinless life
and although He was innocent, He chose to die in my place
so I could belong to You.
I receive the forgiveness Jesus offers me through His life sacrifice
that was offered to pay for my guilt against You.
I receive your invitation to know You.
Thank You for Your Holy Spirit that I welcome to live in me
and baptize me now in Your power so I can live for you,
boldly speak the truth in love, and confirm the Good News in my life
by Your power that Jesus said would be in me and on me.
Thank You for this new life in You
and for the authority and
freedom to live as Jesus did
and for victory over the devil.

Saying this prayer from the heart is the first step in your new life in Him. You have been born again! For the first time in your life, you have come to life the way God intended! Jesus said the angels in heaven rejoice when this happens. Heaven is celebrating over your response to God's goodness and offer of salvation!

Along with *Good Fish* Bad Fish, Kevin Casey is also the author of *Who's Your Daddy*, written to help people live life full of meaning and purpose as the Father intended. Pastor Kevin and his wife Melanie have been married for nearly 30 years and have ministered together since day one God's Good News about Christ Jesus. They understand that as Jesus is revealed, faith springs to life. The abundant life they are living of peace, healing, love, prosperity and freedom bear witness to their message. Their desire is to see people of all walks of life come to receive, know and reflect Jesus transforming them from lost into God's family. They have two adult children are pursuing God's call and plan of goodness in their lives wholeheartedly.

Kevin serves as Pastor of The Father's House in Wise County Texas. Along with his role as Bereavement Coordinator and Hospice Chaplain, Kevin is currently the Regional Advocate for Associated Related Ministries International (A.R.M.I); a support ministry for local pastors sponsored by Andrew Wommack Ministries International.

To connect with Kevin Casey you can reach him at **info@kevincasey.net**.

Tips to Keep You Swimming

Following are helpful tips as well as study guide questions for each chapter to help you dig deeper into living the Good Fish life.

Tip #1: Fish Food

Renewing the Mind with Daily Bread (The Word of God) to Know God and Really Live

"...'People do not live by bread alone, but by every word that comes from the mouth of God.'" —Jesus (Matthew 4:4 (NKJV)

Do you want to know God's perfect plan for your life? Do you want to know His leading with confidence when making important decisions? You can and will if you start each day with a prayerful reading of His Word.

Some read the Word knowing it has truth in it. God wants to take you further than that and allow the Word of God to germinate and live in you. As your inner man steadily beholds the Word it, will transform you. The Word reveals God's true nature and is the authority that gives you confidence to know and trust God in all storms of life.

The Bible is revelation of God. Reading and meditating on it will transform your mind and reveal God's good, pleasing and perfect will. It renews your mind into the mind of Christ. Believing what it says will heal sick bodies and emotions. It divides your soul to separate the right and wrong desires. It develops the eyes and ears of your heart to hear and see the way God intends for us to.

Jesus said, *"Therefore everyone who hears these words of mine and puts them into practice is like a wise man who built his house on the rock. The rain came down, the streams rose, and the winds blew and beat against that house; yet it did not fall, because it had its foundation on the rock."* (Matthew 7:24-25)

A happy, fruitful and meaningful life comes from living out of the right foundation. Hearing, accepting and persevering in The Word leads to a fruitful life. Start each day prayerfully reading His Word and then take it with you in your heart thinking about it all day long.

Tips to Prepare Your Heart

- <u>Find a quiet place in the morning</u> before the distractions of the day start in.

- <u>Pray before you read,</u> asking the Holy Spirit to hear what He is speaking to you through His Word. Resist anything that would try to distract you from hearing.

- <u>Capture the truth</u>. Underline anything that speaks or strikes your heart while reading and/or write in a journal the verse or thought that came to mind. Meditate on these verses throughout your day.

- <u>Listen to the love of God</u> as you read listen to His Spirit with your heart. Be ready for great encounters with Him!

A great place to start with bible reading is the New Testament. Here we become acquainted with Jesus and the New Covenant of grace that Good Fish live within.

Here Is a Plan That Can Help:

Give yourself a timeline for reading through these chapters and mark them off when you've completed your reading.

The Gospels – Four Eyewitnesses To Jesus' Life

John	Matthew	Mark	Luke
Chapters	Chapters	Chapters	Chapters
__ 1-2	__ 1-2	__ 1-2	__ 1-2
__ 3-4	__ 3-4	__ 3-4	__ 3-4
__ 5-6	__ 5-6	__ 5-6	__ 5-6
__ 7-8	__ 7-8	__ 7-8	__ 7-8
__ 9-10	__ 9-10	__ 9-10	__ 9-10
__ 11-12	__ 11-12	__ 11-12	__ 11-12
__ 13-14	__ 13-14	__ 13-14	__ 13-14
__ 15-16	__ 15-16	__ 15-16	__ 15-16
__ 17-18	__ 17-18		__ 17-18
__ 19-21	__ 19-20		__ 19-20
	__ 21-22		__ 21-22
	__ 23-24		__ 23-24
	__ 25-26		
	__ 27-28		

Acts: The Church under the Holy Spirit's direction

Chapters		
__ 1-2	__ 9-10	__ 19-20
__ 3-4	__ 11-12	__ 21-22
__ 5-6	__ 13-14	__ 23-24
__ 7-8	__ 15-16	__ 25-26
	__ 17-18	__ 27-28

Instructional letter's to the Church

Romans
Chapters
— 1-2
— 3-4
— 5-6
— 7-8
— 9-10
— 11-12
— 13-14
— 15-16

1 Corinthians
Chapters
— 1-2
— 3-4
— 5-6
— 7-8
— 9-10
— 11-12
— 13-14
— 15-16

2 Corinthians
Chapters
— 1-2
— 3-4
— 5-6
— 7-8
— 9-10
— 11-12
— 13

Galatians
Chapters
— 1-2
— 3-4
— 5-6

Ephesians
Chapters
— 1-2
— 3-4
— 5-6

Philippians
Chapters
— 1-2
— 3-4

Colossians
Chapters
— 1-2
— 3-4

1 Thessalonians
Chapters
— 1-2
— 3-4
— 5

2 Thessalonians
Chapters
— 1-2
— 3

The Pastoral Letters

1 Timothy
Chapters
— 1-2
— 3-4
— 5-6

2 Timothy
Chapters
— 1-2
— 3-4

Titus
Chapters
— 1-2
— 3 & **Philemon**

Hebrews: Letter to Christian Jews explaining the New Covenant

Chapters
— 1-2
— 3-4
— 5-6
— 7-8
— 9-10
— 11-12
— 13

The General Letters

James
Chapters
__ 1-2
__ 3-4
__ 5

1 Peter
Chapters
__ 1-2
__ 3-4
__ 5

2 Peter
Chapters
__ 1-2
__ 3

1-3 John
__ 1 john 1
__ 1 John 2
__ 1 John 3
__ 1 john 4
__ 1 john 5
__ 2 John
__ 3 John & **Jude**

Revelation
Chapters
__ 1-2
__ 3-4
__ 5-6
__ 7-8
__ 9-10
__ 11-12
__ 13-14
__ 15-16
__ 17-18
__ 19-20
__ 21-22

This is just the beginning. The Old Testament is also full of God's truth and power for living. After completion of this New Testament reading, plan move on to another one that includes the Old Testament. Keep in mind that there is a great difference between the Old and New Testament. But it's not God who changed. We are the ones who changed after being made righteous by the blood of Jesus. The judgment for all of our sins has been taken care of through the sacrifice of Jesus.

So read the Old Testament realizing the people in the stories had a sinful nature and could never really live right or be right with God. God in His love and grace credited Jesus' righteousness to them when they believed Him. They looked forward to the cross while we look backwards at it. At just the right time Jesus came and became our sacrifice to bring peace between God and man by making us righteous before God when we trust in what Jesus did for us. Through your faith in Jesus you now please the Father. The children of God in the Old Testament had hard unbelieving hearts that constantly defaulted to the sinful nature.

When you read the Old Covenant or Old Testament, you will find rich lessons for the New Covenant believer. You must, however, read it understanding you are under a different covenant with your righteousness based on faith in whom Jesus is and what He did and not on your ability to always do the right thing. You will hear His heart for you in the Old Testament through this understanding.

Tip #2: Fish Talk

Make a Good Confession: Your Life Follows Your Words

Did you know you can choose to nourish the way you feel, or you can choose to nourish the way you believe? One way takes no effort; it is a lazy reactive response to the circumstances. There is another way; it is the fight of faith. It takes resolve to speak the truth not from what you feel, but by what you believe.

Human wisdom communicates based on limited information. It operates in our circumstances or emotions. Jesus had spiritual wisdom and his disciples did not. This is why they got upset about not having bread, or the sinking of their boat while they were in it, but Jesus never did. The Apostle Paul explains that spiritual truth, or the Word of God, is higher than human wisdom.

1 Corinthians 2:13-14 says, "When we tell you these things, we do not use words that come from human wisdom. Instead, we speak words given to us by the Spirit, using the Spirit's words to explain spiritual truths. But people who aren't spiritual can't receive these truths from God's Spirit. It all sounds foolish to them and they can't understand it, for only those who are spiritual can understand what the Spirit means." (NLT).

You can trust in human wisdom or you can trust in God's Word. Whatever you trust will direct your life and become your everyday experience. If you are going to live the life of abundance that God has for you (see John 10:10) then you are going to have to trust God's Word. His Word is Spirit and truth. When you speak His Word out loud you are nourishing your trust in Him by reminding yourself of what He has said. This principle is encouraged throughout scripture. For example:

Psalm 107:2 (NLT)
"Has the Lord redeem you? Then speak out! Tell others he has redeemed you from your enemies."

Philemon 6 (NKJV)
"that the sharing of your faith may become effective by the acknowledgment of every good thing which is in you in Christ Jesus."

2 Corinthians 4:13 (NLT)
"But we continue to preach because we have the same kind of faith the psalmist had when he said, 'I believed in God, so I spoke.'"

1 Samuel 30:6 (AMPC)
"David was greatly distressed, for the men spoke of stoning him because the souls of them all were bitterly grieved, each man for his sons and daughters. But David encouraged and strengthened himself in the Lord his God."

Most people understand their thoughts direct their life. As you begin to habitually speak these words out loud over your life each day, you will begin to see your life transform. Your mind has been programmed to believe human wisdom through the world's constant influence and your five senses. It takes discipline and repetition to change your deeply ingrained way of thinking.

Your own voice is the most powerful voice of influence in your life. God's Word coming out of your mouth will go to work immediately to transform your way of thinking and living. You will begin to experience God's good, pleasing, and perfect will for you. As Romans tells us, "Don't copy the behavior and customs of this world, but let God transform you into a new person by changing the way you think. Then you will learn to know God's will for you, which is good and pleasing and perfect." (Romans 12:2 NLT).

This is a whole new way of living. You are using God's Word to transform your thoughts leading you into a closer relationship of trust with Heavenly Father. And when you trust God, all things are possible.

Use the following scriptures to declare out loud the truth of God's Word over your life:

Whatever the Word of God says I am...**I AM!**

I am God's masterpiece.
Ephesians 2:10 (NLT)
For we are God's masterpiece. He has created us anew in Christ Jesus, so we can do the good things he planned for us long ago.

I am God's prized possession.
James 1:18 (NLT)
He chose to give birth to us by giving us his true word. And we, out of all creation, became his prized possession.

I am blameless.
Colossians 1:22 (NLT)
Yet now he has reconciled you to himself through the death of Christ in his physical body. As a result, he has brought you into his own pres-

ence, and you are holy and blameless as you stand before him without a single fault.

I am complete.
Colossians 2:9-10 (NLT)
For in Christ lives all the fullness of God in a human body. So you also are complete through your union with Christ, who is the head over every ruler and authority.

I am chosen by God.
1 Thessalonians 1:4 (NIV)
For we know, brothers and sisters loved by God, that he has chosen you,

I am forgiven.
Colossians 2:13 (NIV)
When you were dead in your sins and in the uncircumcision of your flesh, God made you alive with Christ. He forgave us all our sins,

I am free.
Romans 6:14 (NLT)
Sin is no longer your master, for you no longer live under the requirements of the law. Instead, you live under the freedom of God's grace.

I am right with God.
Romans 3:22 (NLT)
We are made right with God by placing our faith in Jesus Christ. And this is true for everyone who believes, no matter who we are.

I am a child of God.
Galatians 3:26 (NLT)
For you are all children of God through faith in Christ Jesus.

I am led by the Spirit of God.
Romans 8:14 (AMP)
For all who are *allowing themselves* to be led by the Spirit of God are sons of God.

I am powerful since God's power is in me.
Ephesians 3:20 (NCV)
With God's power working in us, God can do much, much more than anything we can ask or imagine.

I am pleasing to God.
Philippians 2:13 (NLT)
For God is working in you, giving you the desire and the power to do what pleases him.

I am dependent on God.
John 15:4-5 (NIV)
Remain in me, as I also remain in you. No branch can bear fruit by itself; it must remain in the vine. Neither can you bear fruit unless you remain in me. *"I am the vine; you are the branches. If you remain in me and I in you, you will bear much fruit; apart from me you can do nothing."*

Whatever the Word of God says I can do...**I DO!**

I do all things through Christ.
Philippians 4:13 (KJV)
I can do all things through Christ which strengtheneth me.

I sincerely call God my Heavenly Father.
Galatians 4:6 (NLT)
And because we are his children, God has sent the Spirit of his Son into our hearts, prompting us to call out, "Abba, Father."

<u>I do the good things he planned for me to do.</u>
Ephesians 2:10 (NLT)
For we are God's masterpiece. He has created us anew in Christ Jesus, so we can do the good things he planned for us long ago.

<u>I follow God's leading.</u>
John 10:3-5 (NIV)
"The gatekeeper opens the gate for him, and the sheep listen to his voice. He calls his own sheep by name and leads them out. When he has brought out all his own, he goes on ahead of them, and his sheep follow him because they know his voice. But they will never follow a stranger; in fact, they will run away from him because they do not recognize a stranger's voice."

<u>I am fruitful for Christ.</u>
Philippians 1:22a (NLT)
But if I live, I can do more fruitful work for Christ...

John 15:16 (NCV)
You did not choose me; I chose you. And I gave you this work: to go and produce fruit, fruit that will last. Then the Father will give you anything you ask for in my name.

<u>I overcome anything that tries to overcome me.</u>
1 John 5:4-5 (NKJV)
For whatever is born of God overcomes the world. And this is the victory that has overcome the world—our faith. Who is he who overcomes the world, but he who believes that Jesus is the Son of God?

<u>I live in peace.</u>
Colossians 3:15 (NKJV)
And let the peace of God rule in your hearts, to which also you were called in one body; and be thankful.

<u>I minister with God's ability.</u>
1 Peter 4:11 (NIV)
If anyone speaks, they should do so as one who speaks the very words of God. If anyone serves, they should do so with the strength God provides, so that in all things God may be praised through Jesus Christ. To him be the glory and the power for ever and ever. Amen.

<u>I always triumph in Christ.</u>
2 Corinthians 2:14 (NKJV)
Now thanks *be* to God who always leads us in triumph in Christ, and through us diffuses the fragrance of His knowledge in every place.

<u>I live by faith.</u>
2 Corinthians 5:7 (NIV)
For we live by faith, not by sight.

<u>I live true life and rule in life through Jesus Christ.</u>
Romans 5:17 (NCV)
One man sinned, and so death ruled all people because of that one man. But now those people who accept God's full grace and the great gift of being made right with him will surely have true life and rule through the one man, Jesus Christ.

<u>I live in divine protection and lay hands on the sick to see them healed.</u>
Mark 16:18 (NLT)
They will be able to handle snakes with safety, and if they drink anything poisonous, it won't hurt them. They will be able to place their hands on the sick, and they will be healed."

I lead others to Jesus as an ambassador and a minister of reconciliation.
2 Corinthians 5:19-20 (NLT)
For God was in Christ, reconciling the world to himself, no longer counting people's sins against them. And he gave us this wonderful message of reconciliation. So we are Christ's ambassadors; God is making his appeal through us. We speak for Christ when we plead, "Come back to God!

Whatever the Word of God says I have...**I HAVE!**

I have gifts from God.
John 17:7 (NLT)
Now they know that everything I have is a gift from you,

I have everything I need.
2 Peter 1:3 (NLT)
By his divine power, God has given us everything we need for living a godly life. We have received all of this by coming to know him, the one who called us to himself by means of his marvelous glory and excellence.

I have the character of Christ or the fruit of God's Spirit residing in me.
Galatians 5:22-23 (AMP)
But the fruit of the Spirit [the result of His presence within us] is love [unselfish concern for others], joy, [inner] peace, patience [not the ability to wait, but how we act while waiting], kindness, goodness, faithfulness, gentleness, self-control. Against such things there is no law.

I have the power of the Holy Spirit to witness.
Acts 1:8 (NLT)
But you will receive power when the Holy Spirit comes upon you. And you will be my witnesses, telling people about me everywhere—in Jerusalem, throughout Judea, in Samaria, and to the ends of the earth."

<u>I have God as my Abba (Daddy) Father.</u>
Romans 8:15 (NLT)
So you have not received a spirit that makes you fearful slaves. Instead,
you received God's Spirit when he adopted you as his own children. Now
we call him, "Abba, Father."

<u>I have boldness and access with confidence before God.</u>
Ephesians 3:12 (NLT)
Because of Christ and our faith in him, we can now come boldly and con-
fidently into God's presence.
<u>I have the peace of God which exceeds anything we can understand.</u>
Philippians 4:7 (NIV)
And the peace of God, which transcends all understanding, will guard your
hearts and your minds in Christ Jesus.

<u>I have redemption through the blood of Jesus.</u>
Colossians 1:13-14 (NIV)
For he (Christ Jesus) has rescued us from the dominion of darkness
and brought us into the kingdom of the Son he loves, in whom we have
redemption, the forgiveness of sins.

<u>I have unspeakable joy and my heart rejoices.</u>
1 Peter 1:8 (NLT)
You love him even though you have never seen him. Though you do not see
him now, you trust him; and you rejoice with a glorious, inexpressible joy.

<u>I have God's love.</u>
1 John 4:16 (AMP)
We have come to know [by personal observation and experience], and
have believed [with deep, consistent faith] the love which God has for us.
God is love, and the one who abides in love abides in God, and God abides
continually in him.

<u>I have the mind of Christ.</u>
Philippians 2:5 (KJV)
Let this mind be in you, which was also in Christ Jesus:

<u>I have all my needs met from His glorious riches in Christ Jesus.</u>
Philippians 4:19 (NLT)
And this same God who takes care of me will supply all your needs from his glorious riches, which have been given to us in Christ Jesus.

<u>I have been given a spirit of power and of love and self-discipline – not the sprit of fear.</u>
2 Timothy 1:7 (NLT)
For God has not given us a spirit of fear and timidity, but of power, love, and self-discipline.

<u>I have Christ in me, the hope of glory.</u>
Colossians 1:27 (NKJV)
To them God willed to make known what are the riches of the glory of this mystery among the Gentiles: which is Christ in you, the hope of glory.

Tip #3: A Good Fish Way to Pray

The J-O-Y-! Prayer

"Never stop praying." 1 Thessalonians 5:17 (NLT)

The JOY! Prayer

Taking time to pray should never be viewed as a Christian duty but a joy. Prayer is a joy because it is an intimate time of fellowship with Him. It is about sharing your heart and listening to His. Jesus taught us to come to the Father using His name to ask for anything we might want. Asking in His name is not just tagging your prayer with, "In Jesus Name, Amen." Using His name is like using the power of attorney for legal reasons. We ask in agreement with His nature and His will. For example, no one may truly ask, in His name, for his neighbor's house or wife. These requests clearly violate His Word, which is His will.

Father wants to work cooperating with you and powerfully through you in this world to do His will. When you pray, you are not trying to desperately move an unwilling or oblivious God to do something in this world. Quite the opposite is true, He is already searching for receivers of His gifts and promises to see His Kingdom come and will to be done on earth as it is in heaven. Grace has given and faith actively receives. Prayer is our way of releasing faith to receive what He has already given through the payment on the cross and the promises He has spoken that are backed up by His name.

A daily prayer time helps me to remember Who He is, what He has said and what He has done. I find that centers my heart and life on Him. My faith grows resulting in worries, fears or anxieties fading. When I pray I am telling my heart about my God instead of about my problem. When I pray in response to a scripture I read or have been meditating on, my confidence rises knowing I have the mind of Christ on my situation. If God worked a certain situation out for someone in His Word, and I am facing a similar situation, He will also do it for me.

When I ask, I am vocalizing my faith to invite Him into the situation and circumstances for His glory. He uses my prayers of faith to give His will voice to accomplish great things. "You have not because we ask not" (See James 4:2) is a very sad scripture.

Here is a simple prayer structure I have followed since I was a child.

The Joy! Prayer structure:

J – is for Jesus. Remember, prayer is a joy because it is an intimate time of fellowship with Him. It is about sharing your heart and listening to His. I begin my prayer time coming boldly to the Father in the position or the name of Jesus to find help in my time of need. I come with thanksgiving and praise for Who He is and What He has done. This is the portion of my prayer time where I focus on praising Him instead of asking from Him. I love to declare His attributes. This reminds me that everything pressing against me is insignificant and impossibilities are simple things for God. As I pray, I pause to listen for His voice and impressions on my heart to follow Him in praying.

O – is for others. This is the time where I lift up the leadership of the country, my church, my family and the needs of others I am aware of. Using scripture is a helpful way of asking in faith. I listen and follow leadings of His Holy Spirit to pray for needs that are impressed on my heart for others.

Y – is for you. At this point I ask and thank God for my needs that have been met through the promises and the payment on the cross but have not been manifested yet in my life's physical experience. Comparatively, a check written from my bank account and signed by me is a promise of payment to whomever it is written, God's Word and promises are real payment spiritually that require faith to be made manifest in the physical world we live in. If I am ignorant of His promises, I will be unable to have faith to receive what I ask for. So I use the Word in asking, and I listen for impressions in my spirit for how to ask and what to ask for along with my petitions I have written down.

Many believers are focused on sin and repentance in their prayer time. This may be why many believers no longer pray and even neglect to simply give thanks for their food before they receive. If you are struggling with an area where your love for God is divided towards a love of sin, by all means, take it to the Father. Forgiveness for your sins past, present and future have been paid in full on the cross. Receive His forgiveness time and time again, and let it stir up thanksgiving and gratitude. I am clearly not saying sin time and time again but if you do sin, do not run from Him instead, run to Him. Deal with it quickly to receive healing and begin to walk into healthy obedient living. In short, your relationship will grow with a time of prayer that is focused on Him and not on you.

! – Praying in the Spirit. At this point, I pray in tongues. Jesus said "this will be a sign for them that believe." (See Matt 28:15-18). The benefits of this practice have already been discussed in the "Flying Fish" chapter. When I do this, I have confidence that I am praying the perfect will of God and I can enter into a rest.

Prayer is not a laborious work but a JOY! This simple structure to my prayer life has helped me to center my heart and life on Who God is, and how much He loves me, have a daily morning conversation where I listen as well as speak in faith, lift up the needs of others with confidence and roll my cares over on to Him because He cares for me.

The aim of this helpful structure to my prayer time is primarily for a morning devotional time with my Heavenly Father through the righteousness Jesus has given me and led by the Holy Spirit. However, the Apostle Paul instructed us to pray without ceasing. This is why throughout the day we lift up praises and requests, trusting Him consciously and constantly aware of His presence and our relationship with Him.

Study Guide and Discussion Questions

Good Fish/Bad Fish
Chapter 1 Questions

1. Jesus' life had been prophesied _____. He even _____. (*Page 5*)

2. Jesus used a fishnet to explain about the harvest, what do you think He might use to help explain about the harvest today? **(Discussion Questions)**

   _____

   _____

   _____

3. If you are only doing good to others and going to church, does that make you a good fish? _____ (*Page 7*)

4. Which type of fish are you? Where will you end up? **(Discussion Questions)**

   _____

   _____

   _____

VIF
Chapter 2 Questions

1. When we sin it _____ our hearts toward God. (*Page 11*)

2. A world without God is an environment saturated by _____, _____, and _____ hearts. (*Page 11*)

3. What may be **the** most referenced scripture in the bible today? _____ (*Page 14*)

4. If Jesus destroyed the works of the devil, should we be able to do the same with Him in us? **(Discussion Questions)** _____

_____

_____

5. How can satan hurt God? _____ (*Page 12*)

6. A bad fish is hooked on what? The _____ of the devil. (*Page 14*)

Fish Follow Their Hearts
Chapter 3 Questions

1. Bad fish may look _____ on the outside but their hearts still _____. (*Page 18*)

2. Will God judge us on the condition of our heart?_____ (*Page 18*)

3. Can a person be so blinded that he does not even realize he is rebelling?_____ (*Page 19*)

4. How can you tell if your heart is healthy? (*Page 21*)

5. What do the Commandments expose to us? Our _____ (*Page 20*)

6. Where does sin begin?_____ (*Page 20*)

7. How can we tell if our heart is right with God? **(Discussion Questions)**

_____

_____

Fishing Must Be Legal
Chapter 4 Questions

1. When Adam and Eve chose to sin, there were _____. (*Page 25*)

2. Did the serpent make Adam and Eve sin in the Garden? Why or Why not? **(Discussion Questions)** _____

_____

_____

3. We need God's standard because we blind to _____ _____ _____. (*Page 26*)

4. Who was sent to deal with sin, once and for all?_____ (*Page 28*)

5. What was the blood of animals used for in the Old Testament? _____
_____
_____ (*Page 28*)

6. The gift of God is free but receiving it is not _____. (*Page 32*)

7. Are God's Covenants permanent or temporary?_____ (*Page 30*)

8. True or False: The Blood of Jesus does not just cover our sins but it washes them away forever?_____ (*Page 31*)

How to Identify a Fish
Chapter 5 Questions

1. Where were some Christians thrown into in the early days of Ancient Rome?_____ (*Page 35*)

2. What sign did early Christians use to identify one another?_____ (*Page 35*)

3. Where is our identity when we are made right with God (righteous before God)?_____ (*Page 36*)

4. True or False: The Bible calls Jesus the last Adam?_____ (*Page 37*)

5. As a believer, your job is to develop your faith by: _____ _____ (*Page 39*)

6. What are some areas that you see in this day and age where people are not being honest. **(Discussion Questions)** _____
_____
_____

The Flying Fish
Chapter 6 Questions

1. True or False: With God, can the impossible become possible?_____
   (*Page 47*)

2. In John 14:12, what kind of works did Jesus say the believer would do?
   _____. (*Page 47*)

3. Why was the Holy Spirit not able to rest on anybody continually before
   Jesus?_____ (*Page 50*)

4. What is the purpose of fasting?_____
   _____ (*Page 50*)

5. Are we made righteous by our own works?_____ **(Discussion Questions)**
   _____
   _____

6. Your new life of faith means you are living a new life of _____.
   (*Page 52*).

7. True or False: When you pray in tongues, you always understand what
   you're saying._____ (*Page 59*)

Deceived Fish
Chapter 7 Questions

1. True or False: A kind person, who does good things but does not believe
   in Jesus, will make it to Heaven._____ (*Page 65*)

2. True or False: People who only trust in themselves are not right with
   God. _____ (*Page 67*).

3. Is there a difference between a born-again person (good fish) that has
   done something wrong, or an unbeliever (bad fish)?_____
   (*Page 67*)

4. What kinds of things do you get absorbed in and distract you from your focus on God. **(Discussion Questions)** _____

_____

_____

5. What does "repent" mean? _____ (*Page 69*)

6. When we repent, what does it bring?_____ (*Page 69*)

7. If we are enjoying sin and God at the same time, what does that make us? _____ (*Page 70*)

8. What makes it possible to be done with sin?_____ (*Page 70*)

9. What truths must you believe in order to transform from a bad fish to good fish?_____(*Page 72*)

How to Stay Healthy
Chapter 8 Questions

1. As a believer are we truly at home on this earth? _____ (*Page 76*)

2. What is the intention of the enemy? _____ (*Page 76*)

3. What is Jesus' intention for us? **(John 10:10)** _____
_____ (*Page 76*)

4. How do you feel the hostile environment of the world keeps you from being mature and fruitful in this life? **(Discussion Questions)** _____

_____

_____

_____

5. What part of God's plan accomplishes reaching the world and encourages the believer to follow Jesus?_____. (*Page 78*)

6. What must church doctrine be based on?_____.
(*Page 79*)

7. What is the only power the devil has today?_____. (*Page 80*)

8. What will transform your mind from bad fish to good fish thinking?_____. (*Page 77*)

9. Your life is determined by what your heart chooses to _____. (*Page 83*)

10. What are the 3 C's that a good fish should avoid?_____, _____, and _____. (*Page 87*)

11. Prayer with understanding takes _____. Praise brings our hearts and minds into correct _____. (*Page 88*)

Just Keep Swimming
Chapter 9 Questions

1. A good fish is also a good _____. (*Page 97*)

2. Neither the _____ nor _____ can force you to follow them. (*Page 97*)

3. True or False: Everyone is lost until they believe and receive Christ as their Savior and Lord?_____ (*Page 97*)

4. No matter how much you look like somebody else, you are still an absolute _____. (*Page 100*)

5. Both physical and spiritual gifts or abilities must be _____ and _____. (*Page 100*)

6. True or False: Whatever you do, should be done for God's glory? _____ (*Page 102*)

7. As a good fish, you have purpose to do _____ works. (*Page 104*)

8. Since you have become a good fish, how have you had miraculous days with Jesus? **(Discussion questions)** _____
_____
_____
_____

9. Eternal life begins when you say, "yes" to Jesus and transform into a _____ fish from a _____ fish. (*Page 106*)

Answer Key

Good Fish Bad Fish Study Questions with Answers

Chapter 1: Good Fish/Bad Fish

1. Jesus' life had been prophesied **before** He even **arrived**.

2. Jesus used a fishing net to explain about the harvest, what do you think He might use to help explain about the harvest today? **(Discussion Questions)**

3. If you are only doing good to others and going to church, does that make you a good fish? **NO**

4. Which type of fish are you? Where will you end up? **(Discussion Questions)**

Chapter 2: VIF

1. When we sin it **hardens** our hearts toward God.

2. A world without God is an environment saturated by **sinful**, **hard**, and **unloving** hearts.

3. What may be the most referenced scripture in the bible today? **John 3:16**

4. If Jesus destroyed the works of the devil, should we be able to do the same with Him in us? **(Discussion Questions see John 14:12 and Acts 10:38)**

5. How can satan hurt God? **By hurting the ones He loves.**

6. A bad fish is hooked on what? **The lures of the devil.**

Chapter 3: Fish Follow Their Hearts

1. Bad fish may look **good** on the outside but their hearts still **stink**.

2. Will God judge us on the condition of our heart? **YES**

3. Can a person be so blinded that he does not even realize he is rebelling? **YES**

4. How can you tell if your heart is healthy? **A life of actions that fulfill the law of God**

5. What do God's Commandments reveal to us? **Our heart's condition**

6. Where does sin begin? **The heart**

7. How can we tell if our heart is right with God? **(Discussion Questions) You have to look at your heart the same way God does.**

Chapter 4: Fishing Must Be Legal

1. When Adam and Eve chose to sin, there were **consequences**.

2. Did the serpent make Adam and Eve sin in the Garden? Why or Why not? **NO (Discussion Question) He deceived them into freely choosing to sin.**

3. We need God's standard because were blind to **our own failures**.

4. Who was sent to deal with sin, once and for all? **Jesus (Hebrews 7:27, 9:26 and 9:28)**

5. What was the blood of animals used for in the Old Testament? **To cover the sins of Israel.**

6. The gift of God is free but receiving it is not **automatic**.

7. Are God's Covenants permanent or temporary? **Permanent**

8. True/False The Blood of Jesus does not just cover our sins but it washes them away forever? **TRUE**

Chapter 5: How to Identify A Fish

1. Where were some Christians thrown into in the early days of Ancient Rome? **To the lions**

2. What sign did early Christians use to identify one another? **FISH**

3. Where is our identity when we are made right with God (righteous before God)? **In Jesus**

4. True/False The Bible calls Jesus the last Adam? **TRUE (1 Corinthians 15:45)**

5. What is your job when you are a believer? To develop your faith by **staying in the Word and renewing your mind**.

6. What are some areas that you see in this day and age where you seen that people are not being honest. **(Discussion Questions)** _____
   _____
   _____

Chapter 6: The Flying Fish

1. With God, can the impossible become possible? **YES**

2. In John 14:12, what kind of works did Jesus say the believer would do? **The same and greater**

3. Why was the Holy Spirit not able to rest on anybody continually before Jesus? **There was not a completely righteous vessel**

4. What is the purpose of fasting? **To know God and to turn down all of the world's distracting voices.**

5. Are we made righteous by our own works? **NO (Discussion Questions)**

6. Your new life of faith means you are living a new life of **obedience**.

7. True or False: When you pray in tongues, you always understand what you're saying. **FALSE (See 1 Corinthians 14:13-14)**

Chapter 7: Deceived Fish

1. True or False: A kind person, who does good things but does not believe in Jesus, will make it to Heaven **FALSE**

2. True or False: People who only trust in themselves are not right with God. **TRUE**

3. Is there a difference between a born-again person (good fish) that has done something wrong, or an unbeliever (bad fish)? **YES**

4. What kinds of things do you get absorbed in and distract you from your focus on God. **(Discussion Questions)** _____
   _____
   _____

5. What does "repent" mean? **Reverse or change your thinking in an area.**

6. When we repent, what does it bring? **LIFE**

7. If we are enjoying sin and God at the same time, what does that make us? **Double Minded and unstable.**

8. What makes it possible to be done with sin? **GRACE**

9. What truths must you believe in order to transform from a bad fish to good fish? **The Gospel message found in our prayer of salvation.**

Chapter 8: How to Stay Healthy

1. As a believer are we truly at home on this earth? **NO**

2. What is the intention of the enemy? **Steal, kill and destroy**

3. What is Jesus' intention for us? **To have a rich and satisfying life (John 10:10)**

4. How do you feel the hostile environment of the world keeps you from being mature and fruitful in this life? **(Discussion Questions)** _____
   _____
   _____

5. What part of God's plan accomplishes reaching the world and encourages the believer to follow Jesus? **The Church**

6. What must church doctrine be based on? **The Word of God**

7. What is the only power the devil has today? **Deception**

8. What will transform your mind from bad fish to good fish thinking? **Prayerfully reading God's Word**

9. Your life is determined by what your heart chooses to **believe**.

10. What are the 3 C's that a good fish should avoid? **Criticizing, complaining and condemning**

11. Prayer with understanding takes **focus**. Praise brings our hearts and minds into correct **focus**.

Chapter 9: Just Keep Swimming

1. A good fish is also a good **fisherman**.

2. Neither the **devil** nor **God** can force you to follow them.

3. True or False: Everyone is lost until they believe and receive Christ as their Savior and Lord? **TRUE**

4. No matter how much you look like somebody else, you are still an absolute **original**.

5. Both physical and spiritual gifts or abilities must be **discovered** and **developed**.

6. True or False: Whatever you do, should be done for God's glory? **TRUE**

7. As a good fish, you have purpose to do **good** works.

8. Since you have become a good fish, how have you had miraculous days with Jesus? **(Discussion Questions)** _____
_____

9. Eternal life begins when you say, "yes" to Jesus and transform into a **good** fish from a **bad** fish.

Diving Deeper—the Good Fish/Bad Fish study questions—are contributed by Marcus and Tricia Draper. You can hear them regularly on their online radio ministry on The Father's House Radio Station at **tfhpeople.com** and online at **themessengersradio.com/radio/**.

Made in the USA
Middletown, DE
25 March 2019